JFK AND BOBBY, ARNIE AND JACK

...and DAVID!

The Unusual PR Career of David Pearson

by David Pearson

RoseDog Books
PITTSBURGH, PENNSYLVANIA 15238

RoseDog Books
585 Alpha Drive
Suite 103
Pittsburgh, PA 15238

Visit our website at www.rosedogbookstore.com

ISBN: 978-1-4809-6981-0
eISBN: 978-1-4809-6958-2

To Anne

"I saw under the sun that the race is not always to the swift…
But time and chance happen to them all."

Ecclesiastes

INTRODUCTION

There are really two parts to this memoir. One is about my experiences with famous people – primarily in politics or sports. I hope these vignettes might amuse, if not enlighten, readers about the circumstances in which a young public relations professional can find himself.

The other is a short version of my life: what kind of a background did a guy like me have that prepared (or didn't prepare) me for dealing with giants like Bobby Kennedy and Joe Di Maggio?

The book starts out with the assassination of President John F. Kennedy. Totally by chance, I happened to play a role in the White House on the night of November 22, 1963. You will learn why I was there, who I saw and what I did there, a witness to History.

David Pearson
June, 2016
Miami, Florida

THE ASSASSINATION

Inside the White House the night of Nov. 22, 1963
(From The Miami Herald Nov. 21, 2010)

By David Pearson

By a twist of fate, Miami native David Pearson —then a Peace Corps press officer, later the operator of a South Florida public relations and marketing firm —was called to help at the White House on the evening of Nov. 22, 1963, the day John F. Kennedy was shot. His observations, first published in 1983, are reprinted here in abridged form, on the eve of the 47th anniversary of JFK's assassination.

She is standing there in that funny posture of hers. Feet slightly apart, arms out from her sides, body tilted forward. Eyes so wide that she looks like one of those Keane paintings, hollow brown eyes fixed on the casket. Unseeing.

She still wears the nubby rose suit, chocolate-colored stains on her skirt where his head has lain.

Right now, in a mixture of dawn and candlelight, this woman I see is not regal or stoic or even in control. She is a grieving young widow bereft of her young husband, and as human as any deeply loving wife.

Minutes later she will be sobbing bitterly, slumped in the arms of her brother-in-law, Bobby.

The world doesn't think of Mrs. John Fitzgerald Kennedy this way. Her collapse by the coffin that night of the murder is but part of the never-before-told story of what really went on inside the White House in those tense, strange hours after sunset on Nov. 22, 1963.

I was there. I tacked black crepe. I fetched sandwiches. I wrote press releases. I emptied ash trays. I ran errands. I also watched and I listened. And I remember what has now become history and legend.

Who was I ... and why was I there? I was a second-level Peace Corps press officer working for Sargent Shriver, and because the White House press staffers were all out of town —Pierre Salinger was flying over the Pacific with some Cabinet members, Mac Kilduff had gone with President Kennedy to Dallas and Andy Hatcher was out of reach—I was tapped to be inside the White House all through that remarkable night. It is 3 P.M. that windy, fateful day. I am frozen at my desk, still stunned with the awful news of John Kennedy's murder in Dallas.

My phone rings. "Shriver wants you and Lloyd Wright to go to Ralph Dungan's office at the White House to help." Running all the way, we are across Lafayette Square and there in four minutes.

When I get to the front gates, I realize I don't have my wallet with my ID card. Lloyd pulls his ID card out and vouches for me. Shriver has phoned ahead, so they let us through. I am surprised because the Secret Service men are running around like squirrels under the trees, and it occurs to me that they are jumpy for nothing. Their president has already been shot.

We slip into Dungan's big office. Seated around the large desk are Shriver, McGeorge Bundy, Arthur Schlesinger Jr., Angier Biddle Duke, Capt. Tazewell Shepard (the naval aide), Maj. Gen. Chester V. Clifton (the military aide) and an Army protocol colonel. Duke has a protocol assistant who looks like Bruce Bennett, and I wonder what he is doing here. Also present are John Bailey, the national Democratic chairman; Ted Sorensen and Lee White and Bill Moyers. Each will play an important role tonight.

The mountains of news accounts of those dark days will tell the world that Jacqueline Kennedy, who "has borne herself with the valor of a queen in a Greek tragedy," as The Washington Star's Mary Mc-Grory would write, made virtually all the arrangements, and that the widow "overwhelmed White House aides with her meticulous attention to the melancholy arrangements that have had to be made." Life magazine, in banner headline fashion, would report that "Mrs. Kennedy's decisions shaped all the solemn pageantry" and would go on to tell its readers that the widow arrived back at the White House at the crack of dawn to personally supervise the arrangements.

For the sake of American legendry it may be just as well for history to continue with this version. One of the requirements of a legend, after all, is that there be as few players as possible to accomplish whatever extra-human deeds need to be done. But it is not a true picture. What my eyes and ears take in tonight is a combined effort by a group of men —men who don't always appreciate each other's offerings, but men who get things done.

It is entirely true that Mrs. Kennedy would impart a number of thoughts and wishes, relayed from Bobby Kennedy to Shriver through continual telephone calls. But it would become clear to us on this sleepless night that the careful details are being accomplished by Shriver and certain other key men who translate her wishes into substance, form and effective action.

I look at these other men, these famous men who knew Kennedy intimately. I am distressed that I keep noticing Schlesinger's crooked bow tie that proves he tied it himself, his baggy suit, the striped shirt.

He looks just like an active historian. And the brilliant McGeorge Bundy (born on Monday, christened on Tuesday, Harvard on Wednesday, etc.). McGeorge Bundy, crisp and nasal. Sleek in an Italian suit with slash pockets, no belt, no cuffs, pointy black shoes and cheap plastic glasses. He has to go soon. He is the White House civilian who must make sure no wrong military word gets out to all those Polaris submarines with the nuclear weapons pointed up.

When the president's jet arrives at 5:58 P.M., Shriver has a long phone conversation with Bobby. Then he turns and says to us, "I'd like you all to know, in a general way, what Mrs. Kennedy's and the family's wishes are. Mrs. Kennedy feels that, above all, those arrangements should be made to provide great dignity for the president. He should be buried as a president and a former naval officer rather than as a Kennedy."

The man is kind and informal but thoroughly decisive. The Catholic hierarchy at this point want a solemn high requiem Mass. Shriver explains respectfully that Kennedy didn't like pomp. He presses for a pontifical requiem Mass — a "low" Mass with restraint, yet one given considerable dignity because it is the Pope's Mass. Like most men in important positions, Shriver frequently turns to trusted aides for information or opinions, even when qualified specialists might be at hand.

Now Shriver speaks to a young psychiatrist, Dr. Joseph English, a close friend who is also a knowledgeable Catholic layman. English's gentle humor is a tonic: "Let's take the low road, Sarge," he says softly.

Shriver decides. "Look, if he made it a point to attend a low Mass himself every Sunday, why should we force a high Mass on him now?" It is a question that calls for no answer. There is none. It will be a low Mass.

I realize now, in the brief silence that follows, that the real protagonist in all this planning is a man who says nothing — John Kennedy. Once the over-all schedule is worked out, it now becomes necessary to tackle the task everyone dreads. Who will be invited? Who are the most honored men in our nation? And who are the president's real friends?

While reading the draft of a press release, Shriver suddenly looks up. "Good Lord, we have forgotten Ike, Hoover and Truman." Shriver quickly jots their names down on the release and turns to Averill Harriman, who is slumped down next to me on a couch. I look at Harriman, at the deep, sad lines in his face. He is surprisingly tall, but thin and somewhat stooped.

"Mr. Ambassador, aren't you a good friend of President Truman's?"

Harriman nods. "Yes."

"Would you please contact President Truman, President Eisenhower and President Hoover and invite them to come tomorrow morning?"

Harriman goes off to make and send the telegrams and returns two hours later to report that Truman and Eisenhower will be there, but Hoover's health will prevent him from attending.

Shriver is, without question, the dominant figure here. Yet when a national magazine is later to publish a detailed account of his life, there will be not even a hint of what should go down as one of the most superb contributions of his career.

The plain truth is that he is more creative than the professionals tonight, more creative than the protocol experts, the clergy, the military and more creative than Andy Hatcher, Lloyd Wright or me with the press.

Adlai Stevenson has just walked in. He is rumpled and pale, more grief-stricken than anyone I have yet seen. He was in Dallas a few weeks ago, was spit on and hit by "hate" placards. But he's alive, and he seems almost apologetic about it. He makes the rounds of the room slowly, speaking to every person, shaking hands.

Some say, "Hello, Ambassador," others, like Shriver, greet him with, "Hello, Governor." He moves to the worn leather couch, sits next to me, and listens for a while. Hearing nothing he wants or needs to hear, he rises slowly with a great sigh and leaves the White House for some less public place of mourning. Throughout the evening the nation's highest public servants continue to check in at the Shriver command post.

John Kenneth Galbraith moves in awkwardly, on legs as long as stilts. He talks in low tones to a few people, sits briefly, then, like Stevenson before him, senses his duty does not lie here and slips away.

Young Bill Moyers, officially Shriver's deputy but actually the strongest link between the two presidential camps, confers with Shriver several times. Mike Mansfield worries through the room and disappears.

Senator Everett McKinley Dirksen flows in, greeting the workers with mellow words: "I still can't believe it has happened; I am stunned, shaken. But thank God there are those like you who are carrying the burden at this terrible time. Is there anything at all I can do to help?" Somehow everyone feels a little better for Dirksen's words.

Dungan's secretary, honey-blond Pat Pepperin, has herded three other secretaries into the outer office, and they are typing up lists of people to be considered. Hundreds and hundreds of names. They are handled quickly, mostly read aloud by Dungan. "Barney Ross," Dungan says. Someone answers, "Yes."

So Ross, an old shipmate on the PT-109 and now a minor government jobholder, will be sent a telegram tonight. But for every yes, there are to be a hundred no's. In addition to the names on the lists, other people throw in names. In the middle of the long chore, Lloyd Wright says: "How about Billy Graham?" There is a pause and Wright adds, "Billy considers himself a close friend of the president."

Another short pause. By now there is real embarrassment in the air. Someone says Graham sometimes played golf with Jack Kennedy. Dungan says simply, "No."

Shriver says nothing.

Next name.

Dungan has the main say-so. He knows more than anyone else whom the president really liked. This is the final test.

Someone mentions George Smathers. Dungan says: "He's a senator, isn't he? Let him come with the rest of the senators."

Yet Byron (Whizzer) White is invited even though he would also be invited separately with the Supreme Court justices.

They aren't all in Who's Who. Some are simply little people the president was drawn to. Like Roy Hoopes, a freelance writer and work-up softball player.

John Bailey, chairman of the Democratic National Committee, keeps throwing up names of old-line pols —people Bailey thinks Kennedy is indebted to because of their help in past campaigns.

Finally Shriver cuts him off. Looking Bailey straight in the eye, he says, "John, we are not trying to return political favors here tonight. We are trying to ask only those people who we know were personal friends of the president."

Bailey only blinks and continues to baldly suggest names of political cronies from New England. Bailey. An angry uncle, rumpled and tired, totally out of place, actively incongruous. A magical facility for saying wrong things at right times.

Shriver remembers that he has called Bill Walton, an artist and close friend of the Kennedys, and asked him to come over. Walton, along with the presidential arts advisor, Dick Goodwin, is preparing the East Room. Shriver asks me to go over and get Walton to see if he knows of any Kennedy friends who might have been left out. I have never been through the inner rooms of the White House, but somehow —I guess it must be from seeing the White House on TV and in pictures —I walk through the many corridors directly to the East Room.

Walton, natty and urbane, is quietly giving instructions to a furniture upholsterer who is up on a 20-foot ladder, hanging black window curtains. Walton belongs at a Palm Beach garden party. Not in the White

JKF and Jackie arrive in Dallas, November 22, 1963

Body of President Kennedy in the East Room of the White House

Jackie Kennedy is escorted by Robert Kennedy and Ted Kennedy. Sargent Shriver walks behind Mrs. Kennedy.

Lyndon Johnson is sworn in as President, flanked by Lady Bird Johnson and Jackie Kennedy.

November 29, 1963

Dear Dave,

I've already told you how much I appreciate the help and support you gave me in the White House last Friday night, but I did want you to hear from me in writing and to repeat once again my gratitude for the way you pitched in.

We couldn't have gotten things ready in time if it hadn't been for people like you.

Sincerely,

Varge

Mr. David Pearson
5312 Sanger Road
Alexandria, Virginia

Letter from Sargent Shriver following the Nov. 22 assassination of President Kennedy and subsequent White House preparations.

House on this blustery November night. Blue blazer, striped tie, flannel pants and polished loafers. Absolutely cool. Talking with him as we go from the East Room back to Dungan's office, I am amazed at Walton's poise. I know he is very close to the president, and especially to Mrs. Kennedy.

It strikes me again that these people for whom Kennedy had such high respect are acting just as he would have wished them to. They have an almost superhuman ability to remain in complete control ... emotions sheathed ... fine and gentle humor ... restraint.

At about 1 A.M. Shriver heads over to the East Room for the first time, followed by Lloyd Wright and me.

On the way through the hollow corridors we pass an open room with a TV set turned on. No one is in the room. The network is running tapes of old Kennedy speeches. Shriver walks into the room, impulsively sits down before the TV set, looks at the screen.

It is JFK's moving Berlin speech. Kennedy says, "Ich bin ein Berliner." The German crowds roar. Shriver gets up, walks out, heading again for the East Room. After a few steps he comes to the president's office, where an armed Marine guard stands by the open door. There is a chain across the opening to the darkened room.

Shriver stops at the chain and looks in. The Marine guard flicks on the light. Shriver stares at the president's empty chair a full minute, then turns and starts to say something to us. All that comes out is a hoarse croak. It is the first time I have seen any visible sign of the deep distress that must be tearing at him.

He quickly turns on his heel and marches down the corridor to the East Room, clearing his throat, squaring his shoulders and staying several paces ahead of us.

I see Bill Walton lighting a cigarette. I walk over and borrow his lighter. Walton tells me of Jackie's request: "She wants the East Room to be prepared for him like it was for Lincoln. If they're going to get here about 2:30, I really doubt that we can match the Lincoln scene by then."

Now, and contrary to later press versions, Walton, Goodwin and Shriver decide not to try to recreate the Lincoln decor exactly. It is felt that heavy black curtains over all the mirrors and crepe drooping over all the chandeliers would make the room too morose and too dark.

Walton and Goodwin are studying an engraving of Lincoln lying in state in the East Room, an illustration in an original copy of Harper's Weekly. (Shriver had gotten the Director of the National Archives out of bed to fetch the antique copy). "They were pretty rococo in those days," Goodwin says. "I think we can capture the right feeling," Walton suggests, "and yet adapt it a little more to Jack Kennedy."

So they simply hint at mourning, draping only the mirror frames with crepe, looping only a single strand of crepe around the center of the chandeliers. I say hesitantly to Walton, "Maybe there ought to be some kind of crucifix." Joe English agrees. A crucifix is sent for, and when it arrives, it turns out to be pretty awful, with a bloody corpus.

Shriver takes one look at it and says, "That's terrible. Go get the one in my bedroom." So we get the Danish modern crucifix from Shriver's home in suburban Maryland. I ask Walton whether the casket will be open at any point. He says softly, "Jack didn't like to be touched. I doubt whether he'd like to be stared at now."

About this time Mac Kilduff, the assistant press secretary who came back with the body on Air Force One, arrives. There is a pause in the preparations while Kilduff gives us a rundown on the events in Dallas. It is the first time I hear that Jackie's pink suit as well as her stockings were splattered with blood.

As the time for the body to arrive nears —it is now scheduled for 4:30 A.M. —Shriver's desire that everything be right extends outside of the East Room to the hall and entranceway.

He has to move furniture from the entrance to make sure there will be room for the pallbearers to bring in the casket. We have already moved a large grand piano out of the East Room, the same piano that was used for several of the Kennedys' musicales.

Pierre Salinger has arrived in Washington and is sitting in his office with his feet up on his desk, a cigar clamped between his teeth, talking to Kilduff and Hatcher, his two assistants.

Now, in the blackest part of the night, just before dawn, headlights begin to cut through the gloom in front of the White House. Most of us, embarrassed and feeling out of place, retreat to a corner of the East Room. Shriver remains at the door to greet the widow and direct the pallbearers.

I hear the routine sound of doors opening and closing, low voices; then come sounds that make me shiver. A military voice snaps a "march" command; there is the clipped staccato sound of boots hitting the hardwood floors. We've been in this hushed and calm house for hours, and now I hear marching....

The Norman Rockwell Marines carry in the casket and set it down on the replica of Lincoln's catafalque. The young priest and two altar boys kneel and pray silently. The pallbearers step back from the casket. There is a short pause; no one quite knows what to do first. There has been no rehearsal. No one has had any experience. What do you do when you bring a dead president into the East Room of the White House at 4:30 in the morning?

The priest walks to the head of the casket, carrying holy water in a tiny one-ounce bottle. He says a couple of prayers in Latin and in English and sprinkles a few drops on the bier.

Now, right in the doorway stands Jackie, with Robert McNamara on her right and Bobby Kennedy on her left. I didn't know McNamara was that close a friend. What a fierce black eagle in a dark suit, his mouth a straight line above the flexing jaw. And still he is tender and solicitous of the widow.

Over to Bobby, stooped and questioning, kind of the way Montgomery Clift used to look. His suit hangs unpressed, his knot off to one side. Stunned, caught out sleep-walking in hell. Will he wake up, will we, and find everything's all right again?

The little altar boy with a candle lighter goes up to ignite the four large candles at the corners of the casket. The wick at the first candle is down under the metal shield; it seems to take him an excruciatingly long time to light. I should run and pull the wick up. I know Bobby Kennedy, another ex-altar boy, has the same thought. But who could go up and ruin the scene? So we wait.

Now I look over at Jacqueline Kennedy, and it seems to me that she appeared out of nowhere, an apparition standing in that characteristic pose of hers that would become so well-known to the world in the ensuing days.

Feet apart, the slight lean forward. Stiff and awe-struck. Her lips are parted slightly. Her eyes are as if she had just been surprised, only they stay that way. A wrinkle of disbelief on her brow.

I look at her suit. I remember what Kilduff has said and am surprised that she hasn't changed clothes. The dark stains are all over her skirt and her stockings. I know it doesn't matter that she hasn't changed her clothes, but the idea gnaws at me, and it is another one of the totally irrelevant thoughts that plague us all through the night.

This acute sense of awareness is heightened, I suppose, by countless cups of coffee and nerve ends that are strung up like guitar strings. I think I know what an LSD trip must be like, with the intense feeling of reality. In fact, the little boy lighting the candles might be taking much less time than I think.

The candles don't smoke. Very expensive beeswax. The priest moves back. He nods to Mrs. Kennedy. She takes the five steps to the casket and quickly kneels down, almost falling, on the edge of the catafalque. Her hands hang loosely at her sides. She lays her forehead against the side of the casket. She kneels there like that for what seems a long time, but it must span no more than two or three minutes. There

15

is dead silence. Absolutely no sound of any kind. The only movement is the dancing of the four yellow flames. The soldiers are statues. The rest of us, motionless, blend into the darkness as if not there. I am almost afraid to breathe.

With her forehead tilted onto the casket, the widow seems like a teenage girl, head against the flank of her horse or something equally dear. And equally mute. She picks up the edge of the flag and kisses it.

Slowly, she starts to rise. Then, without any warning, Mrs. Kennedy begins crying. Her slender frame is rocked by sobs, and she slumps back down. Her knees give way. Bobby Kennedy moves up quickly, puts one arm around her waist. He stands there with her a moment and just lets her cry.

It is a perfectly natural thing for a woman to do. It would only be later, when the world is to perceive her as a regal and strong and almost inhumanly stoic, that I will relive this scene.

Here, by her husband's casket, she is most human; she is grieving; she is wretched. Through the coming days many people would actually wonder whether she could have loved him very much because she didn't seem to mourn the way people mourn who love deeply.

But those of us in the East Room tonight know she did.

Bobby moves her away from the casket. She is led upstairs. They have brought John Kennedy home.

The White House limousine took me home as dawn was rising over the city. I spent that weekend with my wife and the rest of the world, glued to the television.

On Monday, I was back at my desk at the Peace Corps.

Early Days in Miami

To get the major facts of my life on record, I was born 1932 in Bennington, Vermont, my mother Betty's home; my father Colquitt was a Navy doctor at sea with the Pacific destroyer fleet out of San Diego. My mother went home to have me.

A word about my parents. My father's mother, Elizabeth Hatcher, died when he was six years old. He and his sister Bernice spent the rest of their childhood being shuttled between their father's nine brothers' families, mostly on farms in South Georgia. As a result, he grew up to be a quiet, thoughtful man – you might even say taciturn.

My mother, also named Elizabeth (and called Betty), must have struck a chord deep in Daddy's heart, as she was a dark-haired, blue eyed girl with an ample bosom – very much like his mother. She was also a woman with a big heart whom everybody, his family included, loved.

Growing up she taught us to be kind to everyone. When the church called with a child who needed a temporary home, she always took them in. Once we had a little girl named Christina who lived with us for months, while her mother was recovering from polio.

In 1934 as the depression hit rural Georgia hard, my father and his cousins emigrated to Miami. The men became doctors and lawyers, the women nurses and teachers. My great uncle Isaiah T. Pearson was Dade County Superintendent of Schools, his sons Ray and Tillman were judges, and Daddy's first cousin was Dr. Homer Pearson, who it seemed delivered about half the babies in Miami in those days.

My sisters Barbara and Mary Elizabeth and I moved to Miami when my father became the first anaesthesiologist to practice here. We lived in the Southwest section as most of my father's operations were at Jackson Memorial.

My mother, an ardent Roman Catholic, put my sisters and me into St. Theresa's parochial school in Coral Gables. As my parents had talked me into taking accordion lessons, I began taking it to school in the second grade and playing at various affairs. I also sang in a blackface skit entitled "Shortnin' Bread." I was the doctor ("de doctor done said, 'feed dat pickaninnny shortnin' bread!'"). A pretty far cry from the Civil Rights story I would be selling in 1964, huh?

After Daddy took up golf, he joined the Biltmore Country Club in Coral Gables. After school my sister Barbara and I would walk hand-in-hand, first and second graders, down the sidewalk to the Biltmore. We'd change into our bathing suits and run out to the Olympic-size pool, where we would play until Daddy appeared after his round. Then he'd drive us home.

When I was about 12 my father bought us a rowboat with a five horse motor, and we'd go fishing in Biscayne Bay. I distinctly remember one unusually cold winter day we were in a school of mackerel and caught so many we ran out of bait. Daddy said, "they're so frantic, I'll bet they'll bite a piece of cloth." So we tore up a towel and put a strip on the line. Sure enough, they even hit the cloth!

After a while he said, "OK, that's enough. Pull in your lines." We complained that we were still catching fish. "We have enough for dinner," he said patiently. "There's no point in pulling in fish we aren't going to eat."

That was a lesson I taught my own children years later when we went fishing.

Me and the Accordion

During World War II my mother headed up the Red Cross volunteers in Southwest Miami, and we kids collected tin foil from cigarette packages into large balls, which we donated to the war effort. In the fourth grade when I was 11, I played the accordion in the hallway at SS Peter and Paul School, where we awaited bombs that never fell.

When I graduated from a 12-bass to a 120-bass instrument, I began playing and singing on the radio. There was a program on WIOD called "Crusader Kids," sponsored by Knight Paper Company, which had weekly call-in contests for its Saturday talent broadcast. I played on it a few times, finally winning one Saturday after playing and singing "Anchors Aweigh," "The Marine Hymn," and "The Caissons go Rolling Along." You have to remember this was during World War II, and anything patriotic was a winner.

In the summer, we rode our bikes to Shenandoah Park where we played basketball and softball, and on Saturdays to the Parkway Theatre on Coral Way, which had a feature, a "short subject," a newsreel, and a cartoon.

In high school, although I was a diligent but mediocre football player, I did make the basketball team and was a starting at guard for two seasons.

In the 11th and 12th grades, I was class President (you have to remember we only had about 12 boys in the class). A friend of mine, Fernando (Sonny) Cabeza, used to drive me to Miami Beach on weekend nights, where I sang club dates at small hotels like the Shore Club and the Delmonico.

For some now unknown reason, my mother had invited Dr. Albert Kinsey (The Kinsey Report) to dinner at our house. So I wrote an article, "A Teenager Looks at Sex," and after dinner gave it to him to read. The article was pretentious, smug, jejune and stupid, mainly because I knew virtually nothing about sex, except what I had been warned about by the priests who taught Religion.

Dr. Kinsey graciously took the article and said he would read it and get back to me. That he did, and about a month later I got the article back, inscribed "Very well written, Sir! Albert Kinsey."

Summers in Vermont

During the War, mother would save up her gas ration stamps and every summer would drive us in her 1940 Ford wooden station wagon from Miami to Bennington, Vermont, where her parents, brothers and sisters still lived. When I was 14, I spent a few weeks living with my Uncle Johnny, who had a dairy farm, 15 Holstein cows, two draft horses, pigs, chickens, and a border collie mix.

I never knew what real work was until that summer. We rose at 5 am, fed and watered the animals, then walked the 15 cows up a dirt road to the pasture on a hill. Then we went back to breakfast.

All day long we did mostly summer chores: cutting hay with a one-horse mower, raking it into rows with a hay rake, pitching the hay into small stacks, and finally, hitching up the hay wagon to both of Uncle Johnny's burly percheron horses, Buck and Chub, and — with the weekend help of my older cousins, — pitching it onto the wagon and then into the barn for the cows' winter feed.

In the evening we would walk back up the road to the pasture, where the cows were grazing on the hill. Uncle Johnny would let down the two timbers of the gate, and send the dog after them with a "Go fetch!" admonition that sent the collie flying up the hill to encircle the slow-moving cows downward, nipping at the heels of a wandering heifer here and there. We would then walk along with the cows to the barn, where they would all go in; and, amazingly, most of them walked into their own stalls.

Then Uncle Johnny would pull out a stool and a bucket, sit down, and milk every one of them. Occasionally he would squirt one of the teats full of milk into the mouth of the waiting cat by his side. (I tried but never mastered the art of milking).

The big farm and creamery where Uncle Johnny sold his raw milk was called Fillmore Farms, at the base of Mount Anthony. They had a big patio and a dairy bar, and every Thursday night held square dances. Somehow I talked them into letting me join the band (piano, drums, bass, banjo, tenor sax) and play my accordion with them.

Since I played by ear anyway, it wasn't a big problem to learn "When the Works All Done This Fall" and "Honolulu Baby." To this day I remember the songs that were popular that summer, "I Don't Know Enough About You," "Pistol Packin' Mama," and "When the Lights Go On Again, All Over the World."

For the last two weeks of the summer, I lived with my Aunt Agnes, all of whose kids had left home. Her house was close to the baseball field, where I got to play "work up" and perfect my little curl of a curve ball. I loved it, being in a foreign place where I was a stranger from the Deep South.

Camp St. Leo

When I was 13 and 14 I went to camp at the St. Leo's Prep School in Dade City, Florida, in the hills and lakes country north of Tampa. It was run by Benedictine monks – good fellows, all. In my second year there I won several trophies for softball, tennis and best camper. My mother and father had driven up from Miami to attend the final award night event, and they were as surprised as I was when the Camp Director, Father Raphael, kept calling me up to the podium.

The Bennington Year

The following year, when I as 15, I talked my mother and father into letting me return to Bennington and live with my Aunt Agnes. I was in the 10th grade, and it may well have been the best year of my life up till then. I found my first girlfriend (whom I had met the summer before at the square dance). I made the class basketball team. I pitched for the Jayvee baseball team. We won our first game against Drury High, and the next day in the sports section of the Bennington Banner ran a little story with the headline "Newcomer to Ben Hi Hurls 3-hitter." One of the high points of my so-called athletic career.

I really discovered my "new" voice while up there – it had changed to what was then called a dramatic tenor – and sang solos in the annual musical and Christmas concerts.

One night at a Christmas concert, my Aunt Agnes was in the audience when I rose up from the school chorus and walked to the center of the stage. Aunt Agnes said, "My God, what's he going to do?" I sang "O Little Town of Bethlehem." Up to that night she had never heard me sing. No wonder she was shocked.

Back in Miami for my final two years of high school I was editor of the yearbook, a hint as to what my future career as a writer and public relations man would be.

Singing in Manchester

After graduation, I went back up to Vermont, and somehow got a job playing and singing at the Equinox Lodge, a small hotel and lounge in the center of Manchester. I had to write my mother to ship me my white dinner jacket and formal trousers and shoes, which the owner required me to wear. I was to start the day after July 4th (when the "summer season" started in Vermont), and so I had two weeks to learn as many of the popular songs as I could.

During the day when the bar was closed, I went to the piano, turned on the radio, and played and sang them over and over until I had them memorized. I still remember a few of them: "Little Things Mean a Lot," "The Second Time Around," and "Again."

Opening night I was terrified, as the lounge was full of people looking forward to seeing and hearing the guy whose name was chalked onto the bar mirror: STARTING JULY 4. DAVE PEARSON, HIS PIANO AND HIS SONGS. The owner had printed song request cards for the tables and bar. What if I didn't know the song?

The first request came from two gay ladies sitting at the bar: "It Had to be You." Well if you hum that song, you'll quickly realize after the first two bars, the key changes radically a half note. Impossible for me to play.

Somehow I faked my way through it, finished the set, turned on the juke box and fled to the owner's office. "I screwed up," I moaned. "No you didn't," the owner said. "Now get back up there and sing."

So much for my start; not exactly auspicious. As the summer went on, however, I managed to pick up the lyrics and music to a number of then-popular songs, as well as a bunch of standards. "I Only Have Eyes for You," "You Belong to Me," "Love Letters in the Sand," "Embraceable You."

I really had a great time that summer. As I only played from seven to midnight with Sunday off (Vermont Blue Laws), I had every day free. One of the college kids I met took me to the Dorset Field Club, a small private club with four clay courts, a swimming pool and a nine hole golf course. They gave me a "junior" summer membership for only $50. So most every day I was out on the courts playing doubles with the members' sons and daughters.

At Sea and Ashore in the Coast Guard

As the Korean War was just heating up and the draft had been rein-stalled, I followed my friend Fernando (Sonny) Cabeza into the Coast Guard. Goodness knows what I was thinking of – I had completed one quarter successfully (two A's and a B) in my first quarter at Emory University, and college students were exempt from the draft.

I somehow found myself in boot camp at Cape May, New Jersey, where I quickly learned that playing the piano was a pony trick I could use to my advantage. They needed a piano player for their little four piece combo to play at the Saturday night enlisted men's club dance, so I got the job. This did nothing to make me popular with my fellow boots, who were in their racks by 10 pm.

I went on to spend three years in the Coast Guard, first in San Juan at the Coast Guard Air Detachment (search and rescue). I was first assigned to the Naval Commissary, where I got every night liberty. Soon I found a job "ashore" playing and singing at Hotel Normandie in the Voodoo Lounge. The manager insisted in printing tent cards for the tables, one side saying "David Pearson Plays Your Favorite Songs," and the other four lines for guests to write their requests. I still have some of those cards, and I can't believe how corny some of the requests were: "On Top of Old Smoky," "The Tennessee Waltz," and "Margie," were just a few.

Playing at the Normandie every night was an open invitation to me to drink as much as I wanted. At times there would be two or three Cuba Libres lined up on top of the piano.

As I now look back on it after being sober for 34 years (thanks to a lot of great people in AA and a power greater than myself), this was really when I got hooked on drinking. Before that, it was only a couple of beers at home or in Vermont.

Coast Guard Miami basketball team, 1953

SS Peter & Paul High School Basketball team, 1949. David is number 2

St. Peter & Paul Alma Mater

Words & Music by: David Pearson (1950)

David wrote the school Alma Mater in 1950

When the hotel manager put my picture in El Mundo, the daily paper, in ad saying "Now Playing Nightly in the Voodoo Lounge," my Executive Officer, Lieutenant Commander Natwig (later to become a hero beating off sharks while rescuing plane crash victims in the ocean off San Juan) told me it was against Coast Guard Regulations to have a civilian job. So I had to resign. Natwig then put me in for Yeoman's School in Groton, Connecticut, where I spent the winter months of 1951-2.

Groton was really more fun than work, as I was able to take the train down to Manhattan and spend weekends sleeping on the couch in my sister Barbara's apartment (along with her two roommates). I sometimes sang at Asti's, an Italian restaurant in the Village which featured waiters and bartenders singing opera.

One night I sang "Younger Then Springtime" from South Pacific, and was invited to join the table of a rich older woman in fashion named Jane Adler (the mistress of Edward G. Robinson). She sort of "adopted" me, and from then on would take me to such swanky places as Pen & Pencil and Blue Angel to lunch.

After completing Yeoman's School, I was sent back to Miami and assigned to the 7th District Office. I was able to live at home, so I spent a year catching the bus downtown to the HQ office in the Pan American Bank Building, working all day, and drinking every night at the corner bar, The Cork and Bottle on Coral Way.

I spent my third year in the Coast Guard stationed on a ship in St. Petersburg, Florida, The Juniper (WAGL-219). As I was by then a second class petty officer, I was allowed to have an apartment ashore, which I shared with two other sailors. While carousing around St. Pete Beach on the weekends, I was hired to sing at a bar in Pass-a-Grille Beach called the Bella Vista.

They had a violinist and accordionist, so I didn't have to accompany myself on the piano. My pay was $10 a night and all the booze I could drink. That caught up with me one night when I went home with an older German woman vacationing there, and after a few more drinks, passed out at the wheel and crashed my car on the way back to the ship. They took away my Armed Forces Driver License for that. (I should have had a clue, at that point....)

One night I was the guest of a wealthy Atlanta family at The Bath Club, a swanky private club on Reddington Beach. There was a band, and I was asked to sing. I sang Jerome Kern's "All the Things You Are" and it sounded great with a band behind me. Later in the men's room a distinguished looking man walked up to me and asked about my singing plans. I told him I was going back to college after the service, but that I would continue to sing. He gave me his card, DuMont Television Network, Production Vice President.

The spring that my enlistment in the Coast Guard was up. My father bought me a maroon 1950 Ford convertible as a coming home present, and I headed for New York to see if I could find the guy from DuMont Network. I found him and arranged an audition at their studio. Like an idiot, of all songs I chose to sing "That's Amore," a faux-Italian comic song totally unsuited for my Irish blonde looks. Needless to say, they said, "Thanks, we'll call you," and that was that.

The morning I auditioned at the Latin Quarter, a tall young man with a boyish face was entering the club as I was leaving. I stopped and said, 'Hey, didn't I just see you on Steve Allen?" He said, "No, you saw me on Ed Sullivan."

It was Wayne Newton, who was just starting his career. He got the job; I didn't.

After living with my sister Barbara and her husband Garry for a few weeks, I drove up to Vermont and decided to check out the Manchester Inn where I had sung four years before. Although the ownership had changed, the new owner asked me to play and sing a couple of songs – he hadn't hired the summer entertainment yet.

I played and sang for him and his wife, and got the job. A room in the Inn, breakfast and dinner, and $75 a week, plus tips. I played from 7 to 12 six nights a week, Sunday night off.

I joined the Dorset Field Club again as a junior member and spent my summer days playing tennis and hanging around with the kids whose parents had vacation homes in Dorset and Manchester. It was truly a blast.

Back to Emory

When summer ended I returned to Emory and re-enrolled as a second-quarter freshman. As I was a veteran and had the GI Bill, Emory gave me a number of small jobs to earn extra cash. I was the counsellor in Dobbs Hall, a dormitory my father had lived in 40 years earlier while in Medical School – which gave me free rent. I taught classes in tennis and basketball, as well as working in the gym "cage" giving out sports equipment.

The pay was $1 an hour.

With two friends, Hilton Smith and Jim Sturgis, I formed a trio which played for high school dances and fraternity parties on weekends. Some of the pianos were so old and beat up my cuticles were bleeding by the end of the gig.

I also got a job playing and singing at an elegant French restaurant in Buckhead called Remon's.

The first summer vacation I got a job aboard a seismographic ship working off the north coast of Cuba. My high school friend Fernando (Sonny) Cabeza was a diver aboard the ship, which recorded seismographic waves from the underwater dynamite blasts. My job was as an able bodied seaman aboard the 170-foot former Army crash boat.

While working off the Cuban coast we docked the ship in a little town named Caibarien.

We would be out 10 days working, and have four days off ashore. So Sonny and I hired a local driver and his car to drive us to the city of Santa Clara, about an hour's drive inland. The Saturday we got there we learned there was a big dance in an outdoor pavilion. Naturally we attended.

There we met two attractive young Cuban girls; one a first grade teacher, the other a nursing student. We danced with them till the place closed, and then walked them home, promising to return. We never did, although the teacher did write me a year later.

I majored in History at Emory and, thinking I would teach for a career, I applied for and won a fellowship to Indiana University to work on a Master's degree (tuck that away for a little while). I graduated in February of 1958, returned home to Miami, and found a temporary job playing piano in the lounge at the Everglades Hotel on Biscayne Boulevard. I would play from seven to one; occasionally taking my father's boat out into Biscayne Bay. I usually got home about the same time he was leaving for Jackson Hospital for his early morning operations.

(Although he never said anything to me about my late hours and drinking, I know he must have been concerned.)

Cuba and UPI

Being a hopeless romantic and having a couple of more months before school started at Indiana, I decided to go to Cuba and see what the Revolution was like. My father had bought me a Hillman-Minx convertible for graduation, so I drove to Key West and took the ferry over to Havana. After a week or two I found a job as a substitute teacher in a tony private school called Lafayette Academy.

Some of my new Cuban friends introduced me to an Anglo-Cuban amateur theatre group, and I got a part in their musical, "Guys and Dolls."

I met a dark-eyed Cuban girl in the play named Mariana Ramirez-Correa, daughter of a well-known Havana brain surgeon.* She told me she was doing some undercover things for the Fidelistas (most of the younger Cubans were supporters of the revolution at that time), but I really didn't pay much attention.

That is until I was arrested one day and taken to the Cuban version of the CIA, called "SIM," or "Seguridad Internal Militar." After grilling me about what Mariana and her student friends were doing, and realizing I knew virtually nothing, they let me go. But not without agreeing to leave the country.

So once again I got aboard the ferry to Key West. (I may have been the only gringo deported by the Batista government.)

While I was in Havana, the date I was supposed to be in Bloomington and begin my teaching assistantship came and went. I was really having too much fun down there to pay attention. Truth be told, I don't think I really wanted to go back to school anyway.

But I then needed a job. My cousin Buzz (H. Earl Barber) had been a correspondent for United Press in London at the end of World War II. He encouraged me to apply to the wire service (by then renamed "United Press International"), which offered me a job. After they taught me the ropes in the Miami bureau, they sent me to the Montgomery, Alabama bureau as my first assignment.

The good news for me there was that it was just at the beginning of the Civil Rights Movement, with then-Circuit Court Judge George Wallace refusing to turn over the voting records for Bullock County to the Federal agents sent to retrieve them. Covering Wallace and the FBI

*Years later I learned in Miami that Mariana's father had taught a Cuban doctor-friend of ours, Dr. Ramon Montoro, in medical school in Havana. Further, Jose Bolado, a men's shop owner in Coral Gables, had made Mariana's father's suits when he was a young tailor. I later heard Mariana had married an officer in Cuban intelligence, but nothing more.

32

was heady stuff. But the bad news for me was that my Bureau chief was a heavy drinker whom I would join nightly, listen to Tchaikovsky's Violin concerto, and drink.

As it was my job to open the bureau at 5:30 am to put the weather over the wire for the area radio stations, it was important I got up about 4:30 am to make it in time. One night I stayed out late drinking on a date with the Alabama Lieutenant Governor's daughter. The next morning was the opening of the state Legislature, and it was important that I be in the bureau early. Of course I didn't wake up and around noon that day there was a knock on the door.

After several months of boozy nights and hung-over mornings late for work, this was the last straw. Don Martin, my bureau chief and drinking buddy, handed me the fatal termination letter.

I was devastated. I had never lost a job in my life – and this was the beginning of my professional career! Drinking had always been part of my persona since the Coast Guard days (I called it "port and starboard drinking: drunk one day, hungover the next"). I was humiliated and depressed.

It was too embarrassing to go back to Miami and face my family. So I drove to Atlanta, where I had made a number of friends while at Emory. One of them introduced me to a friend of his who had a PR firm, a big, friendly Virginian named Hap Moore. He hired me, and thus my career split off from pure journalism into public relations.

Sea Pines Plantation on Hilton Head Island

One of our clients was a new resort community development on an island off the South Carolina coast called Hilton Head. The resort, Sea Pines Plantation, was the brainchild of then-29-year-old Charles Fraser, who with a couple of his Yale classmates was developing the island with a concept revolutionary for its time, the precourser ot many of today's ecologically-planned coastal resorts.

Although it may sound extravagant when you first think of it, there's a distinct possibility that Charles Fraser's visionary master plan for Sea Pines may someday rank with Fredrick Law Olmsted's plan for Central Park, Lord Oglethorpe's design for Savannah and Major Pierre L'Enfant's layout of Washington as one of America's seminal land planning efforts.

Fifty years after Fraser's original concepts began taking shape along the pristine slate-gray beaches of Hilton Head Island, the Sea Pines resort has become one of America's favorite family vacation and second home communities.

The planning and design principles he espoused, put carefully into practice over the original 5,200 acres of timberland, marsh and beaches, have been emulated and exported not only to other areas of the U. S., but also throughout the world.

Consider this.

Before Sea Pines, families at most seaside resorts usually had to cross busy roads to get to the beach. Invariably access roads ran parallel to the beach. In the Sea Pines plan, the access loop road was pulled back several hundred yards. One got to the beach via 50-foot-wide walkways on either side of small, discrete vacation home subdivisions sited inside cul-de-sacs. Thus children staying in the house furthest from the beach had free and open access to the ocean, without ever having to cross a road.

Those walkways also provided easements of view as well as breeze corridors for non-oceanfront houses.

Charles' groundbreaking land plan was actually created by a small dedicated team consisting of himself, the famous land planner Hideo Sasaki, and John Wade, one of his young Harvard associates. In 1959 it received the A.I.A.'s first-ever Gold Medal award for land planning.

Basing his philosophy on the writings of Julian Huxley – essentially that wilderness and raw nature are essential to man's wellbeing – Fraser's mantra was "one acre of open space for every acre developed." To ensure that this would be the core of his community, he created a large wildlife preserve in the center. Rife with native birds and deer, feral pigs and alligators, the wildlife refuge and Fraser's conservation principles attracted visitors and buyers of an intellectual bent.

In addition to the land plan, a groundbreaking set of architectural restrictions and covenants were created to run with the land. These rules alone had an enormous effect on future developments, both resort and suburban.

In the ensuing 50 years between then and now, the Sea Pines principles of resort development have been emulated and imitated throughout the world.

Consider these innovations from the original Sea Pines plan:

- No beach homesites beyond the natural dune line
- No roofs visible above tree canopy
- No trees cut larger than 16 inches in diameter
- All residences sited for minimum impact, and to avoid blocking views of other houses
- All residences must be approved by review board (example: no stucco, no clothes lines, no pastel colors, garbage and drying yards mandatory)
- New resort vernacular design developed by architects Wade, Pete McGinty and Tom Stanley
- Two-square-mile wildlife preserve
- Covenants quote Julian Huxley on necessity of wilderness to man's wellbeing

Other innovations included building the resort's hotels outside the gates, creation of bird and wildlife sanctuaries, siting golf holes for natural drainage and minimal tree loss, building of beach clubs for interior residents, creation of upland harbors (Harbour Town, South Beach Marina), innovative home and villa rental programs.

Charlie's innovative group team began with his Yale Law School classmates John McGrath and Lamar (Pete) Caudle along with Wade and McGinty, David Pearson, Wally Butler and Chuck James.

As their successors continued to develop and expand the original plan, Sea Pines grew into a major family resort destination, largely oriented toward sports and nature. Pete Dye and Jack Nicklaus' Harbour Town golf course attracted the national PGA tour, Stan Smith's tennis complex lured the WTA and network television, two marinas attracted both sailing and cruising craft as well as providing eco-type activities such as kayaking and birding.

Exporting the revolution

The Fraser team's first effort to replicate the Sea Pines design principles was at Amelia Island in Florida, a natural paradise which has become one of the most popular resorts on the Eastern seaboard (Sea Pines alumni Jim Rester, Jack Healan and Ralph Simmons ran Amelia). Amelia retained our firm twice, the second time to help them celebrate their 25th anniversary.

Then came Palmas del Mar in Puerto Rico (Fred Sanchez); Kiawah in Charleston (Pat McKinney and Ron Royal); Brandermill in Richmond (Harry Frampton); Snowmass in Colorado and Spring Island in Beaufort (Jim Light and Jim Chaffin). Starting with him back at the Sea Pines headquarters, Charles' other protégés who have gone on to fame in their own right include Phil Lader, Rich Marr, John Gettys Smith, Tom Gardo and Peter Rummell.

Perhaps the strongest river of influence in carrying the original Sea Pines principles to resorts and suburban developments throughout the world has been the ULI, the Urban Land Institute, whose seminars, meetings and publications have extolled and exported the revolutionary planning and design messages through its Resort Development Council. As the words on Charles' tomb at Harbour Town's Liberty Oak say,

> "Design professionals acclaim Fraser as having had a greater beneficial input on policies than any other man in America in the 40-year period following World War II. To see a true memorial to this man, look around you."

Marketing with Smoke and Mirrors

As Fraser had little money to promote Sea Pines, it was up to us to figure creative ways to get the story out to the public. With little experience in PR and marketing, I had to try different things.

Knowing from my UPI days that pictures with animals and pretty girls in them always got great play, I set up a shot on the golf course featuring our "pet" alligator, a 12-foot-behemoth we called Albert. I asked one of our secretaries to put on some Bermuda shorts and stand by the edge of a fairway lagoon holding a five-iron. Then I lured Albert over with a chicken wing attached to a long cane pole.

As the photographer set up his camera, we put a golf ball on the edge of the water, and had the model standing a few feet away, as if she were approaching the ball. Into the frame we lured Albert. When he was in the right spot, the photographer yelled "Now!" and I conked Albert on the head with the pole.

At that he opened his mouth wide, and we snapped the shot. It looked as if Albert was about to gobble up the golf ball (or the model).

I wrote a short piece to go with the picture called "The Golf Course with the World's Greatest Hazards," describing the course and the adjacent nature preserve with its gators, feral pigs, whitetail deer, wild turkey and other wildlife.

I was able to get the picture and the story onto the UPI wire, and as they might say today, it "went viral." It appeared all over the country and even as far as Stars & Stripes in Korea.

We soon decided we needed a color film to illustrate the beauty of the island. Having no money, we went to the tried-and-true Charles Fraser Barter Technique, trading a couple of fairway lots to a Columbia, S. C. film production company for a 25-minute movie.

A property owner named Charles Pelham had been a big-time ad executive on Madison Avenue, and Charlie roped him into helping us. Quickly seeing we had no ad funds, he said we needed to get some national exposure. He set up three days of meetings in the Lincoln Building in New York, to which he invited editors he knew from several of the major media. As we had the half-hour color movie, we would show the editors in, give them a cup of coffee or a drink, and have them see the film before any discussion was held.

That scheme worked, because most of them said, "Wow, I had no idea there was anything so beautiful down there. And the way you're doing it – extraordinary."

Out of that trip we wound up getting major articles in Sports Illustrated, the New York Times, the Daily News, Town & Country and others.

The Sports Illustrated part deserves a brief detour. The Managing Editor, Roy Terrell, called and told me to talk to his editor in charge of the swimsuit issue (now known as their Bathing Suit issue), Fred Smith. I invited Smith to come down and see the resort, but he was very busy and constantly on deadline. I despaired of ever getting him to an out of the way place like Hilton Head.

He told me he was flying to Atlanta soon to visit his mother in Alabama. So I flew to Atlanta, intercepted him when he got off his New York flight and threw him onto a chartered Piper Cub which took us to the island, landing on the grass airstrip on the north end.

One look at the broad beaches, tall pines and new George Cobb golf course, and an evening listening to the dreams of Charles Fraser, was all it took. The result was a major article in Sports Illustrated by Houston Horne with photographs by the now-famous Elliot Erwitt.

We used reprints of that story for years.

The Saturday Evening Post story was actually a two-page photograph of Charles Fraser and Albert the alligator. A Post photographer came down to shoot Fraser for a series called "People on the Way Up." He wanted Charlie in an interesting location. Golf course? Too boring. Beach? Ordinary. Hmmm.

Enter Albert, who had already proven his photographic appeal. We somehow roped the giant gator up out of his lagoon and transported him across the road to the golf clubhouse lawn. There, we put a chain leash around his neck, and let him go. He turned and slowly started walking back toward the lagoon. Fraser, dapper in a Brooks Brothers suit, straw hat and brief case, picked up the leash and strolled alongside Albert while the photographer took the picture.

Needless to say the picture and Charlie's story got great play in the Post, and became an instant legend on the Island. If you visit Hilton Head, you'll see a bronze sculpture of Charles and the alligator on Pope Avenue in a little park.

One day I told Charles I needed a new typewriter. He said, "You do? Go sell a lot."

Another day a Savannah developer named Bill Lattimore asked me if I would moonlight for him and promote his new real estate development. I asked Charlie. "Hmm," he pondered, then said "you keep half and give half to Sea Pines. That way we both make some money."

The first year our golf course and 80-room oceanfront inn were open, we had virtually no business. So I coaxed a few dollars from the company and ran some small ads in the Wall St. Journal. We used headlines like NO NEON! playing up our uncrowded beaches. The next

GREAT EXPECTATIONS

A consultant in the resort and real estate field sees a banner year ahead—especially if you follow his advice!

A conversation with David Pearson, President of Pearson, McGuire, Ruthfield Associates of Coral Gables. Some of David's clients are: Amelia Island Plantation, Boca West, Cheeca Lodge, Longboat Key Club, Palm Beach Polo & Country Club, The Vintage Club, and Jupiter Hills Village.

New Yorker advertising promotion piece featuring David and Sea Pines ad's headline ran GNO GNATS! That one told about our unusual insect control program tied to our conservation ethic. We ran it in the Journal and Natural History as well.

Neither one pulled that great.

So we finally decided to go for broke and advertise the unbelievably low price. Again using the Journal — and although it's hard to believe this - we actually advertised a rate of $13.50 per night per couple!

That little ad got us through the tough winter of 1960.

Meantime I married a girl from St. Louis, Anne Bates, whom I had met during our college days, and we built a house near the beach. A year after we were married, we were expecting our first child. Anne has a story about having that baby which tells a lot about her life with a PR man.

As I indicated earlier, we had precious little capital to promote the development, so we had to use every opportunity get our story out.

During the Civil War, Hilton Head Island had been the headquarters of the Federal blockade (Department of the South). On November 7, 1861, six thousand Union troops stormed ashore on the island in the greatest amphibious landing prior to World War II. So naturally, we thought of re-enacting that famous landing on Hilton Head Island, drawing attention to the island's rich history (not to mention its current resort development).

We were able to convince the Marines on nearby Parris Island to land on our wide beaches, jet fighters from Savannah's Hunter Air Force Base to "strafe" the shore, and the U. S. Army Armored Division stationed at Fort Stewart, Georgia to send some artillery.

Anne was in the labor room in Savannah's Memorial Hospital having Christopher, our first child, when the phone rang by her bedside. "Hello," she answered weakly, in the throes of labor. "Hello Anne," said John McGowan, a Sea Pines salesman who was helping me with the reinactment arrangements. "When you see David would you please tell him we were able to borrow the folding chairs from the Bishop?"

Ever since then Anne has said that not even being in labor took precedence over a phone call about business.

Of course no one could figure out how to get to Sea Pines from anywhere. So it was Charlie's idea to put up directional signs at every intersection between the Savannah bridge and the island. Our Harvard architect John Wade designed a series of colorful wooden arrows on white poles, pointing to SEA PINES PLANTATION; while another would say HILTON HEAD ISLAND. We even put our competitors' names up: PORT ROYAL PLANTATION.

It was my job to find the owners of the property, mostly small African-American farmers, where we wanted to locate the signs, get them to sign a one page agreement, and pay them $15 a year. The first few were easy: here's $15 for doing nothing, they thought. The closer I got to the island, the more I ran into "heir's property." That was property that had been passed down from Reconstruction times, owned by a parcel of cousins, aunts and grandmothers. Many of whom lived in other states.

My solution to that was to pay the first relative I found, and get him to sign the release saying, "ACCEPTED ON BEHALF OF THE XYZ FAMILY."

My big promotion to VP Marketing and Public Relations came one day after John McGrath walked into my office asking to see the marketing plan. "What marketing plan," I said, knowing no such thing existed. "Well Jeezo-Peezo," McGrath allowed, which for him was very close to cussing.

So I had to write one. It is long lost, of course, but if memory serves it included an actual media budget.

Robert Mitchum and Cape Fear

Maybe the best picture Robert Mitchum ever made was "Cape Fear" with Gregory Peck and Polly Bergen, filmed in its entirety in Savannah. As I was the PR man for Sea Pines on nearby Hilton Head Island, I had the idea of inviting the cast to the resort for the weekend. Mitchum and child star Lori Martin took me up on it. Lori rode horseback on the broad lowcountry beach, while Mitchum went fishing on John Mc-Grath's charter boat, The Adventure.

Later over cocktails with the development team, Mitchum invited me to visit him on the movie set in Savannah.

On the agreed day I arrived at the downtown park where the movie was being shot. When Mitchum saw me, he called me over and we both went to lunch in a nearby cafeteria. I remember he ordered she crab soup. Our booth was next to the waiting line, and two older Savannah matrons were leaning over the divider, evesdropping on our conversation. Without missing a beat, Mitchum suddenly inserted a stream of blue language into the story he was telling me. When the first "bastard" came out, the ladies jumped a foot, shocked, and quickly moved away from our booth.

"That's how I get rid of nosy people," he said calmly.

As he wasn't in any more of the day's shots and had the afternoon off, we went to his suite in the nearby De Soto Hotel. The lanky Mitchum lay on top of his bed while I sat in a chair facing him. For the next three hours we drank beer while he regaled me with story after story of Hollywood – making movies on location, gossip about other stars, what he had learned as an actor – including a very sad story about his early years.

At one point in his youth, Mitchum wound up in Savannah and got himself picked up by the police. As he didn't have a job, a home address or a driver's license, they threw him in jail as a vagrant. "I was actually on a chain gang," he reminisced, "stripes and all. I guarantee you it was no fun. So I've been here before, under slightly different circumstances," he said.

That evening we went to dinner along the Savannah Riverfront, joined by his strapping 6'4" bodyguard, whom he called his assistant. Why he needed one became apparent after an hour of drinks, when a nearby patron, obviously plastered, began to harass Mitchum with remarks like, "You're not such a big deal." When it became impossible to ignore the guy any longer, the bodyguard simply walked over, picked him up, and walked him on tippy-toes out the door.

"A typical dinner out," Mitchum said. "Welcome to being a movie star."

On to Washington

My wife Anne and I had two children in Savannah during these years, and we built a home near the Ocean. We had friends and relatives visiting us on weekends throughout the year, one of whom was Doug Kiker, Washington Bureau Chief of the Atlanta Journal, and his wife Ruth.

When he was named Director of Information of the Peace Corps, Kiker called in several of his friends from the Journal to staff his office.

He called me one day. "You've got to come up here," he enthused. "You and Anne would love it here! This is where all the action is. Everything in government is new!"

I wasn't sure whether or how long I would last if I even got a job in the New Frontier, but Charles Fraser, himself a risk taker, said he would give me a two year leave of absence if I wanted to go.

So I went.

And met Sargent Shriver. We bonded immediately. "I don't have a slot for you right now," he told me, "but you're the kind of guy we need in this administration. I'm going to send you to the White House and see if they have something for you

So they introduced me to some men who headed up JFK's new agencies. One, called The White House Study Group for a National Service Program, was under the aegis of Bobby Kennedy and its employees were paid by checks from the Department of Justice.

There was a spot for an information officer, and I was hired. The group's job was to create the social legislation that would later become the core of LBJ's Great Society. But because of a coalition of Southern Democrats and Conservative Republicans, JFK couldn't get anything through Congress. The stumbling block was Kennedy's Civil Rights Bill.

I spent six months as information officer for the Study Group, a combination of lobbying the House and generating favorable press for the proposed legislation.

Former Navy Captain William Anderson headed up this Study Group. He had been the skipper of the USS Nautilus, the nuclear submarine first ever to dive under the North Pole. He was a friend of Bobby Kennedy's, who brought him in to head up what was to be the domestic version of the Peace Corps.

Like most of the positions in these new agencies and task forces, mine was amorphous, shifting almost daily from working with the press trying to place stories about our plans for what eventually became the Vista Volunteers, the Job Corps, Head Start and other Great Society programs.

Nevertheless we pushed on, trying to convince the majority to override the coalition of southern and Republican congressmen to vote for our bill. In a plane lent to us by the Department of Justice, we flew several congressmen out to Pine Ridge, South Dakota, to see first hand the appalling conditions under which the Oglala Sioux were living.

Our plans called for domestic peace corps volunteers (later, Vista Volunteers) to work on these reservations in early childhood education, alcohol and drug rehab, and job training. From there we flew to the Menninger Clinic in Olathe, Kansas, to see their innovative new programs working with developmentally disabled children – programs we wished to bring to other institutions working in urban slums and ghettos.

Bobby Kennedy and the Today Show

One of my goals was to get national exposure for the National Service Program legislation, a subject which usually put reporters for the big newspapers and magazines to sleep. I had become friendly with Martin Agronsky, head of the Washington bureau of NBC's Today Show. He was a huge JFK fan, and considered me typical of the new young New Frontiersmen lured to Washington by his magical "Ask Not" philosophy.

I asked Agronsky if he would interview Captain Anderson on the Today Show to describe our plans for the new agency. "I will if you get Bobby Kennedy to go on with him," Agronsky answered, knowing that the Attorney General was the Study Group's godfather.

Realizing I had a slim chance of getting Bobby Kennedy to do the interview, I nevertheless called Ed Guthman, Kennedy's press secretary, and asked anyway. Agronsky had given me a Monday morning date to shoot at, a month away, for the 7 A.M. interview. So I asked Guthman if Bobby would do it.

He said he would ask, but don't bet on it. I told him I would give him three weeks to let me know one way or the other, and if I didn't hear from him by a week before the show, I would assume RFK would be there. Guthman said ok.

Three weeks later I had not heard from Guthman. So taking a leaf from the Kennedy-style book, I told Agronsky to assume Bobby would be there, as the deadline for declining had past.

The following Sunday morning Bobby's picture was on the cover of the Washington Post's television section, with the cutline saying that he was scheduled to appear on Monday's morning's Today Show with Captain Anderson and Martin Agronsky.

Guthman called me at home early that Sunday morning, apoplectic. "Why the hell did you tell Agronsky the Attorney General would be on his show," he screamed. "This will be my ass, and probably yours too!" I reminded him of our agreement that he would get back to me in three weeks, and that he had not called, triggering the "OK" button.

The next morning was cold and rainy. At 6 am, when we were to meet at NBC, it was still dark. As I sat in the cafeteria drinking coffee with Agronsky and Captain Anderson, the door opened and in walked Bobby Kennedy in a wet trench coat and no hat. He was not smiling.

Agronsky and Captain Anderson shook hands with him. I stood quietly aside. Kennedy looked at me coldly as Agronsky said, "And this is..." before he could finish, Bobby said, "So, ah, you're, ah, David Pearson," in that Boston Irish accent of his. I was instant toast.

Nevertheless, the interview was a great success. Bobby made it very clear this legislation meant a lot to him and to the President, and that it would be evidence that America was finally going to mobilize against the appalling poverty in most of our cities.

When we visited Congressmen that week, we found to our delight that a number of them and their staffs had seen that Today Show interview and were ready to talk to us about the new legislation.

President Kennedy's Press Conference

Seeing the effectiveness of national television first hand, I decided to go for the brass ring: the President. JFK had initiated a series of weekly press conferences from the White House, in which he discussed candidly the issues and problems of the day with the Washington press corps.

Having met Peter Hackes of NBC News and knowing that he was privately a big supporter of the New Frontier programs, I called him and asked if he would be willing to ask a certain question if he were called on. "What? Are you trying to plant a question for the President?" His tone made it clear that he had never done this before, and was unlikely to do it now.

I asked Hackes to think about it, that I was going to get some information over to him about the National Service Program. A few days before the press conference, Hackes called me and said he would do it, but that if I told anyone he would have my head. I gave him the question to ask.

I then called Lee White, one of the President's Special Assistants, a young lawyer whom I had met recently. "No one has ever done this before, to my knowledge," White said, uncertain of the reception he would get from the President if he suggested it. After considering it for a few minutes, he said, "Bring me over two answers. One long one, and one short one." So I wrote the question:

"Mr. President, some people are saying your National Service Program with a domestic peace corps working in mental hospitals and on indian reservations would take the place of the many church volunteer organizations already doing that. What's your answer?"

Short answer: "Peter, those who say that don't understand that our domestic peace corps would supplement, not replace, our charitable organizations. This is a chance to let our young people serve those less privileged – the many who are mired in poverty and despair."

Long answer: "Peter, those who say that haven't seen the abject poverty at the Sioux reservation in Pine Ridge, South Dakota...and they haven't visited any of our many understaffed, underfunded mental hospitals lately. Believe me, the churches and other charitable organizations need all the help they can get, if we're going to help millions of Americas escape a life of poverty."

On the day of the President's next press conference, Captain Anderson, staffer Gerry Studds* and I went to a nearby bar which had a
big TV screen. The one hour press conference was to start at 1 pm. By
1:45 the President hadn't called on Hackes. Then, just as we had about
given up hope, with only a few minutes left, he came through.

"Yes, Peter," he said, pointing at Hackes among a sea of raised
hands. And Hackes asked the question. In answering, you would have
thought Kennedy had never heard the question. He seemed outraged
at the idea that anyone would be against his proposed volunteer program. He took off with my long answer, and added a few choice words
to go with it. Whew.

As with the Bobby Kennedy Today Show appearance, the following
day our phones were ringing off the hook – reporters and correspondents
wanting updates on the bill's passage through the House and Senate.

(*Studds later became a very effective Congressman from Boston,
and was the first to come out as homosexual.)

At the Peace Corps

Shortly after that Doug Kiker called and said an opening had developed
for a Deputy Director in his Public Information Division. He reintro-
duced me to Shriver, who quickly learned I was raised Catholic (plus),
played tennis (plus), and knew the difference between Andrew Wyeth
and Giotto (big plus).

So I became number two in an office where 15 writers and staff
were serious about three-quarters of the time. The successful Peace
Corps story, no surprise, wasn't that hard to sell to the media. It was at
this point the only clear Kennedy success, other than the Nuclear Test
Ban Treaty with Russia. The other quarter of our time was spent thinking up jokes and pranks worthy of a Saturday Night Live script. Some
examples:

- The Gang. Apropos of nothing at all, Jim Walls, a former San Francisco Chronicle arts columnist, came up with a fictitious gang one day while having lunch at the French restaurant on the corner. Eggs Benedict was the Brains of the Mob, Cherries Flambe The Moll. Oysters Rockefeller was a Rich Kid Gone Bad, and Chicken Tetrazzini was The Snitch. Finally, Beef Stroganoff was The Enforcer.

  Walls did not drink. One day I asked him why he didn't eat his dessert, Rhum Baba. He replied that if he took one bite he would wake up two weeks later in Acapulco.

- The Red Phone. Doug Kiker, my boss, had a red phone on his desk. The line went only to Shriver's desk. One Friday afternoon as the whole office was celebrating a big story we had gotten in Look Magazine, I slipped out the door and went down the stairs to Sarge's office on the floor below. Sarge and the secretaries were gone for the day; the door was unlocked.

  I picked up the red phone on Sarge's desk and punched the button marked "Kiker." I later learned that when the red phone rang, Kiker fell out of his chair trying to answer it. "Yeah Sarge," he said breathlessly. "Doug," I began, trying to imitate Shriver's inimitable Maryland accent, and then I collapsed in a fit of laughing.

  Silence on the other end, and then "PEARSON, YOU BASTARD!"

- We had hundreds of head shots of the various Peace Corps country directors around the world, along with their bios. One slow news day, Mort Engelberg, one of our most talented writers (later a Hollywood producer) cut out the eyes from the picture of the Peace Corps Director in Ghana. He then made a Xerox copy of the picture, switched the eyes and pasted them back on backwards, and then Xeroxed that picture. I can assure you there was something very strange looking about the doctored photo.

We photocopied the picture into various sizes and placed it in various places around the office. We put it on the bottom of the large glass government-issue ashtrays, so it was looking at you as you mashed out your cigarette. We put it in the middle of the wall clock, so it looked as if this guy was staring down at you. We found some very inventive uses for it.

One day, of course, the million to one shot happened: the guy from Ghana walked into our office. Panicked, we quickly closeted him with Kiker, closed the door, and frantically dashed around removing his picture from ashtrays, clocks, etc. It may not read funny here, but I can tell you at the time it was hilarious.

Travels With Sarge

One of my press officer jobs was to occasionally travel with Shriver on his recruiting trips to colleges and universities around the country.

Before my first trip with Sarge, several people in Public Information and Public Affairs who had travelled with him previously came to my office to warn me of his distinctive proclivities:

- Shriver is a very sharp dresser, and his suits always look as if he had just had them pressed.
- He doesn't smoke
- He goes to mass every morning no matter where he is
- He doesn't like to lose in touch football

On the morning of my first trip as his press aide, I was to meet Shriver at Washington National for an early morning flight to Chicago. My wife Anne dropped me off at the airport, where I found him checking in at the counter. Together we walked toward our concourse when we passed a small restaurant. We went in, and Sarge ordered and devoured a breakfast of bacon, scrambled eggs, toast, orange juice and coffee. Having eaten at home earlier, I ordered coffee.

After we boarded the plane and reached a stable altitude, the flight attendant took our orders. Sarge ordered another full breakfast. I ordered coffee.

After she brought the breakfast trays, Shriver tucked right into his plate of ham and eggs. As I was lifting my coffee from the flight attendant's tray, the plane took a slight jolt and I spilled it all over the front of my light beige cotton suit. Sarge looked over and said, "holy shit."

As we had a very tight schedule, there was no time to have my suit cleaned until that night at our hotel. So at our appointments all day here was the impeccable Sargent Shriver, followed by his wretched, wrinkled and stained press aide.

At the Chicago hotel, our rooms had connecting doors. That evening as we were getting ready to go to a banquet where Shriver was speaking, I tapped on his door. When he opened it, his mouth full of toothpaste, I asked him if he had a match. "I don't smoke," he burbled, and closed the door.

Shortly after we returned to Washington, Sarge and his wife Eunice invited my wife Anne, me and our children out for a Sunday lunch and touch football at Timberlawn, their rural Maryland estate. After lunch, I joined Sarge's opponent's team in the touch football game on the lawn. Once we scored a touchdown, and as our team remained at that end of the field, I looked at Sarge and said, "sucker's walk." It was, of course, traditional that the scoring team stayed where they had scored, and the opponents had to walk the length of the field to receive the kickoff.

"We're staying here," Shriver averred. "But we just scored!" I said. "Yeah, but it's my field," he answered.

Abroad With the Peace Corps

My only regret during my Peace Corps time was that I travelled a lot, and because of that I had to leave Anne at home with two children, both under two. That got even more difficult for her when she had our third child, Katie, at George Washington Hospital.

All of we senior officers had to split up the national recruiting duties, visiting top colleges and universities signing up Peace Corps Volunteers. I was sent to UCLA and Stanford in California; and Indiana and University of Chicago in the Midwest.

As I was a writer, I was part of a team that went to Cuzco, Lima and Arequipa, Peru; thence to Quito, Ecuador. There we "de-briefed" the PCVs who were about to finish their two-year tours of duty. The idea was to let them vent to officials from Washington, which they were all to ready to do. On our return to the States, I would write a report to Shriver and Moyers stating their complaints and recommendations for improvements in the program.

My last trip was to Aden, Arabia (currently part of Yemen and under attack by ISIS terrorists), de-briefing a contingent of PCVs from Somalia. As there was trouble in Somalia, the Peace Corps was recalling them early, before their two years were up. They were furious, as they had to leave projects they were working on in a number of villages – digging new wells, installing sanitary sewers, teaching English, etc.

I wrote an article called "The Peace Corps Volunteer Returns" that was published in the Saturday Review. One of the more interesting points made by Dr. Joe Colman, a Peace Corps psychologist, is that the Volunteers who had less-than-perfect teenage years at home and in school coped with the difficult conditions they found in the barrios and slums overseas. As compared to the BMOC-type All-

American kids, many of whom couldn't deal with poverty and came home early.

Bill Moyers

Public Television journalist and commentator Bill Moyers, who became a friend during this period, had an interesting background. As a young theology school graduate from East Texas, he had been working for one of Ladybird Johnson's radio stations. He was picked by LBJ to advance his presidential campaign, and became close to the Johnsons on the campaign.

When Johnson became Vice President, he asked Moyers what he'd like to do. Bill said he'd like to serve in the new Peace Corps with Sargent Shriver. So he became Shriver's Deputy, and of course the rest of his career is history: Special Assistant and Press Secretary to President Johnson, Publisher of Newsday, star of Bill Moyers Journal on Public Broadcasting Service, author of several best-selling books.

Sarge and LBJ

Once travelling with Sarge, we were combining recruiting with speeches, one of which was in a small town in Minnesota and there to join Senator Hubert Humphrey at the State Fair. Just before we boarded our Lake Central DC-6 at the local airport, we went into the newsstand where each of us bought a paperback (Sarge's was Barbara Tuchman's "The Guns of August").

As we passed a pay phone, Sarge said to me, do you have a dime, I just spent my last change on that book. So I gave him a dime and stood by while he looked in his little black book for a phone number. He then spoke for a few minutes and then we boarded the plane.

As we lifted into the sky, he looked at me and said, "Here's something for you to remember. That call was to Lyndon Johnson – today's his birthday. I doubt if anyone else in the family is going to call and wish him a happy birthday. Little things mean a lot."

What we didn't know on that summer day in 1963 was that three months later Lyndon Johnson, then Vice President, snubbed and made fun of by most of JFK's staff, would be President of the United States.

With Johnson on that Air Force One flight from Texas to Washington was young Bill Moyers, Shriver's Deputy at the Peace Corps, but a close personal advisor to LBJ. A few days after he took office, Johnson called Shriver to the Oval office where he and Moyers were waiting. "Sarge, you have always been a faithful friend," the President said. "What would you like to do?"

"I'd like to run your new War on Poverty," Shriver answered, referring to the most important part of his new Great Society legislation. Moyers asked, then who will run the Peace Corps? "I'd like to keep the Peace Corps too," Shriver replied. And so it was that Sargent Shriver continued on as head of JFK's Peace Corps, while taking the leadership of Johnson's new poverty program. (Moyers, by the way, never left Johnson's side, becoming his trusted advisor and press secretary).

LBJ, Bill Moyers and Doug Kiker

One day Moyers, by now fully ensconced in the White House as LBJ's Special Assistant, arranged to have the first group of Peace Corps Volunteers to complete their two year service honored in the White House Rose Garden. It was a gorgeous spring day in 1964, and the Volunteers, a few staff members and the press corps were outside waiting for the President to appear.

Sargent Shriver introduces David to President Johnson in Rose Garden in ceremony celebrating return of first Peace Corps contingent after two years in Colombia.

David with Sargent Shriver at Miami International Airport on a recruiting trip for Peace Corps volunteers.

Senator George Smathers, Governor LeRoy Collins and JFK at 1960 Democratic Convention.

David with Presidential Assistant Bill Moyers at Rose Garden ceremony.

John F. Kennedy receiving the Domocratic Nomination for President at the 1960 Convention. To his left is former Florida Governor LeRoy Collins, Convention Chairman.

David entertaining at an Emory Players cast party.

A rostrum with the presidential seal had been set up, and Doug Kiker*, always the clown, walked up to it, hunched over in LBJ style and said into the microphone "I guess you're wondering why I gathered y'all here....." At precisely that point behind him the door to the east portico opened and the president and Bill Moyers walked out. Seeing Kiker at the rostrum, they paused until he finished.

Then LBJ walked to the rostrum and said, "I want to thank Doug Kiker for calling you all together here...."

*Doug Kiker had left his job as Peace Corps Director of Public Information to become the Washington Bureau Chief of the New York Herald Tribune. He took the job just before JFK's fatal trip to Dallas – and was with the press entourage at the assassination. He later became a correspondent for NBC News.

Civil Rights

In July of 1964, Congress finally passed the Civil Rights Act, the bill JFK had tried and failed to get through during his time in office. In pushing it through a still-recalcitrant Congress, Johnson called it a fitting tribute to the fallen President.

One night while I was in Atlanta making a speech about the Peace Corps to an editors convention, I got a note that former Florida governor LeRoy Collins wanted me to call him right away. Although it was 10 at night, I returned his call.

"David," he said in his warm southern way, "the President has given me a big responsibility in the new Civil Rights Law, and I need your help. Can you meet me tomorrow night for dinner in Georgetown?

The next night over dinner in a small French restaurant, Collins told me the story. He had become nationally known after his able running of the fractious 1960 Democratic Convention in Los Angeles. At the time, the big television networks were under attack for a number of reasons – violence in children's programming, cheating on quiz shows. To assuage some of the attacks and improve their image, the networks brought in LeRoy Collins to head of the National Association of Broadcasters, their face to the country. Squeaky clean Collins could polish up their image.

What they hadn't counted on was Collins' strong conscience and fiery rhetoric. Instead of tamping down the fire, he threw kerosene on it by openly decrying the graphic violence and crime dominating much of the networks' programming. The industry was stunned. What had they wrought in bringing Collins aboard?

At that point, LBJ called Collins to a private meeting in the White House. "Roy," he said, grabbing Collins' elbow and pulling him close, "the country needs you. I need you. The Civil Rights Act calls for a new agency, the Community Relations Service, to help achieve peaceful integration in the country.

"I can't have just anybody running something as sensitive as that," he said to Collins, pulling him even closer. I need somebody who knows the South, but knows that segregation is wrong. I need you, Roy."

Collins told him he knew the government job wouldn't pay much; that he was making a big salary running the NAB and had just bought an expensive Georgetown home and had kids in school. The President said let me worry about that, Roy. And without telling Collins, Johnson got hold of the heads of NBC and CBS and told them the situation. Eager to get rid of the outspoken Collins, the two network giants quickly suggested they continue Collins' salary for the length of his contract. Problem solved.

Not being able to turn down the President after that, Collins moved quickly to staff up his new agency with people he knew would believe in social justice, and who would be loyal to him. As his deputy he brought in Harold Fleming of Atlanta, who had been running a civil rights foundation. He also brought in John Perry, a journalist he had known as Florida governor when Perry headed the Tallahassee bureau of the St. Petersburg Times.

And finally, to be Assistant Director for Public Affairs, he came to me, a fellow Floridian.

When I went to see Shriver to tell him of my decision to go with Collins, Sarge said, Gee, I thought you were going with us to Poverty. (That's the first I had heard of that). I told him I thought Collins, with no federal government experience, needed me more. When we parted, I had a premonition I hadn't seen the last of Sarge – and I hadn't.

Sidebar: Dick Goodwin, Le Roy Collins and the Networks

Roll the tape back to the Democratic Convention of 1960, a raucous affair until the calm, elegant Florida Governor, LeRoy Collins, brought it to order. It was Collins' first appearance on national television, and he was very impressive.

Enter Richard Goodwin, then a young Harvard-trained attorney working for the House Oversight Committee. Working on a tip from a former contestant on the NBC quiz show "21," Goodwin revealed that the network and the show's producers had been giving the answers to Charles Van Doren, who was winning thousands every week.

The full story came out at the Congressional hearings, and the television industry took a right to the jaw. (Goodwin was the same young man we will see later working at the White House for JFK and LBJ).

The networks went to work trying to assuage the damage to their images. That's when they hit on the idea of bringing in squeaky-clean LeRoy Collins as President of the National Association of Broadcasters. If anybody could polish up Network TV's image, Collins could.

What the network moguls didn't count on was Collins' intrepidness, and his courage. Right away he began making speeches calling for less violence in television, castigating his bosses for the lack of strong values in their programming.

No surprise, then, when LBJ called the networks and asked if they would continue Collins' NAB salary while he served the nation, they jumped at the chance to get this viper out of their bosom. And Lyndon, being the ultimate arranger, had his man.

Getting the Word Out on Civil Rights: The Community Relations Service

My job with LeRoy Collins at CRS was paradoxical. On one hand we were bound by a rule of confidentiality regarding our mission in mediating racial conflicts – expected mainly in the South. On the other, we were charged with explaining the new law, and gaining its peaceful compliance, throughout the country.

Although my lips were sealed regarding the trips our racial conciliators made into places like Bogalusa, Louisiana and McComb, Mississippi, where the Klan and White Citizens Councils were still very active; I was able to mount a positive program through a cooperative and willing national media.

There were some sidelights:

When putting together a discussion for a national cable network, I had some difficulty locating a well-known conservative journalist willing to appear with the pro civil rights liberals I had lined up. On the plus side I had of course LeRoy Collins; Bayard Rustin, the controversial Black socialist philosopher; Bill Moyers, Special Assistant to the President, (now) Congressman John Lewis, then a young Atlanta Civil Rights leader, and Ivan Allen, progressive mayor of Atlanta. When he heard that Bayard Rustin would be on the panel, Richmond News-Leader syndicated columnist James Kilpatrick refused to appear.

We finally found a conservative journalist willing to enter the lion's den in Holmes Alexander, a nationally syndicated columnist who had opposed the Civil Rights Act from the beginning. Needless to say with that lineup, poor Holmes wound up as toast.

Collins was of course a perfect symbol for the new Civil Rights push. Formerly a courageous Florida governor who at one time had supported segregation, subsequently changed his views and now believed strongly that the doctrine of "separate but equal" was wrong. He thus represented the possibility of the South waking up to the injustices of segregation, and accepting the new Civil Rights Law as a necessary and moral solution.

Selma

I had promised Collins I would give him a year, and I did. It turned out to be a historic year, with Collins' role in the March on Selma, an event resulting in ramifications no one could have predicted. After the first march across the bridge, the police had turned back Martin Luther King and his procession of young protesters with clubs and dogs. Determined not to be denied again, Dr. King planned a second march.

This time the President heard about it in advance, and called Collins. "Roy," he said, "you need to go down there yourself and make sure none of those kids get hurt."

The next morning when we came to work, Collins told us he was going to Selma to meet King and his fellow marchers. He told me to prepare an announcement and run it past the President before releasing it. I did that, and the President's press secretary, George Reedy, told me to go ahead and release it myself.

Of course what Collins did in Selma was the apogee of his courageous political life. He met with King and arranged for the marchers to stop halfway across the bridge, and kneel to pray. He then met with the Selma Mayor and Police Chief and got them to agree to allow the march to the halfway point; that they would stand by and take no action against the marchers.

When the march started, Collins was in the first row, holding hands with Martin Luther King on his right, and Jesse Jackson on his left, leading hundreds of young men and women, black and white, to the middle of the bridge, where they stopped, knelt, sang and prayed.

Although Collins was praised throughout the nation as a man of courage and resourcefulness, a picture that was taken of him walking with Dr. King turned out to be the dagger that mortally wounded him in his 1968 Florida race for the Senate. Florida was still a southern state, and his opponent used the picture to fan the flames of racial hatred that still simmered there.

As a note of the cruellest irony, Collins was defeated, and never ran for office again.

A Conciliator Heads South

One of Governor Collins' key racial conciliators was a big African-American man from Chicago named Abe Venable. After he returned from a particularly arduous and scary trip to Mississippi, he told us this story. (Although it is obviously apocryphal, Collins used it over and over in his speeches from then on):

"I was driving from St. Louis on my way to Mississippi, and as I got deeper and deeper into the South I began to worry about the Klan and the recent murders down there. At one point a thunderstorm arose with lightning and thunder crashing around. 'Lord, look after me when

I get down there among those rednecks,' I prayed, 'cause to tell the truth, I'm scared.'

"Just about that time there was a tremendous clap of thunder and a deep voice came down from above saying, 'Abe, I'll be with you as far as Memphis.'"

Strange Bedfellows

There were many strange bedfellows in the Civil Rights days. LBJ had created a national Council on Community Relations, to which he appointed both political friends and potential enemies, as well as avowed advocates of integration. One of these was a big donor to the Democratic Party, a multi-millionaire from New Jersey named Charles Engelhard. He owned mines in South Africa, and was one of the country's top diamond importers.

Engelhard asked the Governor what he could do to help, and Collins quickly suggested he fund a documentary film he wanted the agency to have. Engelhard agreed, and the job fell to me to produce the film.

I had met Pare Lorentz, Jr., son of the famous documentarian who had produced "The River" and other prize-winning films. Pare and I took the train to New York and met Engelhard's man at the Waldof-Astoria, where he kept a luxurious suite. "You two can stay here tonight," our host told us, as he showed us through the apartment. At one point he opened the drawer of a polished mahogany wardrobe, filled with new cashmere Brooks Brothers sweaters of all different sizes and colors, still in their wrappers.

"If it gets chilly," he said as he left the room, "help yourselves to one of these sweaters."

(The brass plaque above the door to the suite said "Cole Porter Suite." The composer had lived here for years at the end of his career.)

LBJ's Southern Governors to the Rescue.

Shortly after the Civil Rights Act was signed in July of 1964, President Johnson called together three former southern governors who were serving in his Administration. Concerned that he would lose the South in the upcoming election against Barry Goldwater – and that southern Democrats would defect because of his leadership in getting the Civil Rights bill through Congress – LBJ pulled his "southern team" together.

He told LeRoy Collins, former Florida governor and newly appointed Director of the Community Relations Service (CRS); Luther Hodges, former North Carolina governor and now Secretary of Commerce; and Buford Ellington, former Tennessee governor and now Director of the Office of Emergency Services (now known as FIMA); that he wanted them to visit nine southern governors and make sure they didn't bolt the party in the coming election.

Specifically, Johnson wanted them to know that with the passage of the Civil Rights Law setting up the CRS to "ram it down their throats;" that it existed to help them keep peace in their states as the new law was unfolding throughout the nation.

So shortly after receiving their orders from the president, his trio of southern surrogates were in the sky aboard his Jetstar, flying around the South meeting with the governors of nine states. As I was handling the media for Collins and the team, he brought me along as the single staffer on the trip.

My two jobs were to handle any press that might have gotten wind of this "secret" mission, and to record the conversations the trio had with each governor.

Basically the trip was a success. With the exception of Governors Connelly of Texas and Farris Bryant of Florida, each of the other seven governors accepted the President's message with good graces, and pledged to lead his state in peacefully adhering to the new law.

On our return from the first trip to nine governors, I had the task of writing the final wrap-up memorandum, "eyes only" for the President, which I hand-delivered to Lee White, Special Counsel to the President, at the West Gate of the White House.

(Ultimately we visited 26 states and met with the governors of each.)

Bill Moyers, LBJ, and Viet Nam

After spending the year I'd promised Governor Collins at the CRS, my wife Anne and I decided it was time to leave the government and head back to the private sector. When I called Bill Moyers, LBJ's special assistant, to tell him I was leaving, I also asked him how, knowing that he was against the War, he could be a spokesman for LBJ and defend his position.

His answer to me: "David, if I left this job, do you think Lyndon would go out and find someone opposed to the War to replace me?

Years later when Bill was in Miami for the Book Fair, promoting his just-published book, "Genesis," Anne and I met him at the airport and took him to our home for lunch. She had made a chicken and potato casserole, which we ate at the kitchen table. After a while I asked him why he left the White House to become Publisher of Newsday. He smiled ruefully and said softly, "I'm going to tell you two something I have never told anyone before. One morning one of my children was sick and I was late getting to work. There was a cabinet meeting early that day, and when I arrived I kind of snuck into the room, hoping nobody would notice me.

'There he is,' the President boomed out to the surprised cabinet officers, 'ban the bomb Bill!.'

At that moment I knew I was gone."

Art Linkletter, a fan, and David

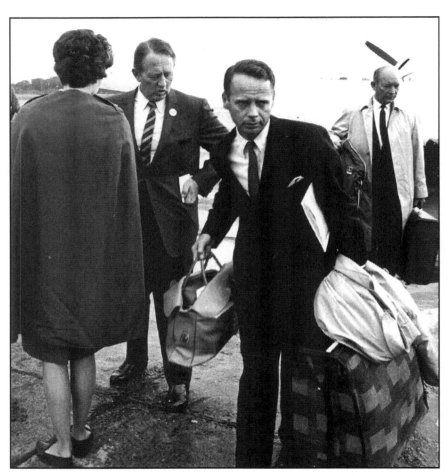

Classic picture of a PR man: David schleps radio and TV star Art Linklet-ter's luggage while on a nation-wide appearance tour for RC Cola.

The Braves (and David, Anne and the now three children) Move to Atlanta

Anne and I decided to move to Atlanta, where I had been offered a very good job with Bell & Stanton, a national public relations firm. I learned a lot about the profession that year, working under Pulitzer Prize-winner George Goodwin.

We settled into a lovely old brick home on Lullwater Drive, just a few blocks from the Emory University campus where I had gone to school.

Almost immediately I was assigned to handle the new Atlanta Braves, who in 1965 moved from Milwaukee. It was a thrill to meet and watch Hank Aaron, Felipe Alou, Tony Cloninger, Rico Carty, Eddie Matthews, Joe Torre and Phil Niekro, not to mention their color broadcaster Dizzy Dean and announcer Milo Hamilton.

One day while travelling with owner Bill Bartholomay, he asked me if I would consider a job in PR with the Braves. I was flattered, but turned him down.

I worked on four clients that year: the Braves, the Atlanta Chamber of Commerce, a sportswear company called Gamewinner, and RC Cola. One of my responsibilities with RC was to figure out how to use their spokesman and shareholder Art Linkletter. Art, famous for his radio shows and his book "Kids Say the Darndest Things," had a contract that called for him to provide 30 days a year promoting RC products.

The company had just rolled out their new "Diet Rite" cola, the first diet cola on the market prior to the entry of Diet Coke. Target markets were women and young people. So we developed a program for Art to go around the country making appearances before women's groups, and speaking at the Business Schools of various colleges and universities.

73

When speaking to business school majors, he would frequently point at me, standing in the back of the auditorium, and say, "There's an example of entrepreneurism: this young fellow, David Pearson, who now works for a national PR firm, is planning on leaving soon to open his own firm in Miami. That's the route to take: learn from the masters, then strike out on your own."

We travelled to Knoxville where he appeared before 1,200 women, followed by a lecture with business students from the University of Tennessee. With the women's groups his subject was always children, while with the students it was America's free enterprise system (Linkletter was a conservative Republican, constantly trying to convert me from my liberal Democratic politics). At each stop, there would be at least 10 or 15 pink phone message slips. Although he didn't return any of them, he did take a call now and then from a local woman – when I pressed the phone on him.

We travelled to San Francisco, Los Angeles, Chicago, Dallas and Philadelphia that year. Maybe not entirely due to "The RC Art Linkletter University Series," their new Diet Rite set sales records across the country.

When the Braves moved into the new Atlanta Stadium, they awarded the soft drink concession to Coca Cola. After failing to convince the Braves they ought to give RC equal space for their products to be sold and being turned down, RC decided to sue Coke and the Braves under the Sherman Anti-Trust Law.

Their position was that the Atlanta Stadium was located at the crux of two interstate highways (I-75 and I-85), and thus was subject to federal oversight as a result of interstate commerce.

Much to my surprise and my employers' chagrin, I was subpoenad to appear before both sides' attorneys for the upcoming trial. Although my testimony didn't prove anything specifically, it did corroborate RC's claim that Coke had the clear competitive advantage. The court ruled that the Braves had to allow RC and other soft drinks into the stadium on an equal basis.

Following my testimony, we had to make a decision whether to stay with the Braves or RC Cola. The firm chose to stick with the Braves, no surprise, so that was the end of my RC days with Art Linkletter and Diet Rite.

During my time in Atlanta I served on the Southeastern Board of the American Friends Service Committee, working especially in their efforts to end the Viet Nam war. While doing this I met and became friends with Julian Bond, whose activities both with the Students Non-Violent Coordinating Committee (SNCC) and anti-war demonstrations had kept him from being seated when he was elected to the Georgia Legislature.

(Our friendship has continued until his untimely death. I had only recently seen and talked to him at the University of Virginia, where he was teaching a course in Civil Rights History).

Laurance Rockefeller, Arnold Palmer and the Caribbean

My former Sea Pines associate and friend John McGrath had left there shortly after I did to take a position with Laurance Rockefeller's new resort organization. John allowed that if I would leave the national PR firm I was with and go on my own, Rockefeller would buy half my time. He gave me the choice to live in New York, Miami, or San Juan. As Miami was my original home and my parents were still there – by that time Daddy had become Chief of Anesthesia at the new Baptist Hospital — my wife Anne and I chose to move the family to there and open my office.

John's first job was to develop a golf course community called Fountain Valley in St. Croix. He brought me in to do the marketing and public relations – my first account as well.

As there were no homes, real estate or hotel built yet, only a new Robert Trent Jones golf course, it was not an easy job to put Fountain Valley on the map. As in the Sea Pines experience, I had to dig deep into my bag of tricks find something promotable and memorable. For the first year, it was mostly using my golf magazine contacts to do fashion shoots over the course. Then one day I heard that John had been able to talk his Republican Party friends into bringing the National Governors Conference to Fountain Valley for a major outdoor event on the golf course.

The Governors of all 50 states were having their annual conference aboard a cruise ship, when was slated to dock in Frederiksted, a few miles from the course. The Rockefeller staff were able to bring top culinary talent from their resorts around the world – Maua Kea Beach, Caneel Bay and Woodstock – and I was given the task of finding the entertainment.

It is somewhat ironic that I, a Kennedy Democrat and obvious liberal, put together a show that featured perhaps the most conservative, right-wing, Republican artists in the business, who just happened to be right for the event.

As MC and the major star, I was able to get my old client Art Linkletter from Hollywood. For the music, we brought down the popular songstress Anita Bryant (whose famous "Battle Hymn of the Republic" brought down the house), The key speaker was Ronald Reagan, then Governor of California, resplendent in a white cashmere jacket.

After Fountain Valley, I was able to bring Little Dix Bay, Caneel Bay and Dorado Beach Hotel to my Rockefeller portfolio. Now I needed the other half of my income. Using that illustrious name as my entre, I was able to sign up Lost Tree Village in Palm Beach and The Deerwood Club in Jacksonville.

McGrath had also been a partner of Mark McCormack, founder of the worldwide IMG sports network, and while with Mark he han-

Rockresorts' PR man Glenn McKaskey, Touring Pro Chi Chi Rodriguez and David on the East Course at Dorado Beach, Puerto Rico.

Former touring star and golf course designer Raymond Floyd with David and Anne Pearson during the Doral Open. Floyd had just remodeled the famed Blue Monster and Gold courses.

David at Fountain Valley on St. Croix, 1967

David at Fountain Valley, St. Croix, in 1967

dled Arnold Palmer's business affairs. Thus it was that I was introduced to Palmer, wrote another of Esquire's annual golf articles about him, and subsequently handled his Bay Hill Club and Resort for two years.

By 1971 I began writing speeches and articles for Brown Whatley, Chairman of the new Arvida Corporation, who were developing Boca West, Sawgrass and Longboat Key Club. One by one I was able to add them to my client list.

Big Three Golf

As Palmer, Nicklaus and Gary Player were all clients of Mark McCormack's. IMG had created a network television event called "Big Three Golf" in which they played against each other. After a season of matches at courses around the world, they were all tied; so a playoff was necessary. John McGrath arranged to have it telecast on the famous Robert Trent Jones, Sr. East Course at Dorado Beach.

Naturally, I had to go down to Dorado to help with producing the event. The night before the playoff round was to be shot, Palmer, McGrath and I drank, hit the casino, and danced until the wee hours. Player never left his room; Nicklaus, after choosing milk over champagne at dinner, retired early.

The next day the Big Three played their round, which took all day because the cameras had to be moved after every shot. Player shot 74 and was out. Palmer and Nicklaus tied at 71 and went head to head in a sudden death playoff.

The sun was setting as Jack and Arnie teed off on the dogleg right par four first hole. Palmer split the middle of the fairway; Jack pulled his deep into the palm trees. Palmer knocked his approach to mid-green, lying two; Nicklaus had to pitch out from under the trees, now lying two in the fairway.

Jack pitched to three feet – now he's at four. The best he could do then was make bogey five. Arnie stroked it to six inches and tapped it in for a four. Game, match, Big Three Championship.

Host pro Chi Chi Rodriguez led the gallery in celebrating Palmer's victory with the resort's signature pina coladas and a swinging salsa band. Nicklaus zipped back to his villa, threw his bags into a hotel limo, and took off in his private jet stationed nearby.

Later than night after many pina coladas Palmer took some of the partiers for a spin over San Juan in his Lear Jet before winging his way back home to Bay Hill in Orlando.

And while I'm on Arnold Palmer, let me jump around in time and recall the several times we crossed paths.

I had written a six page story in Esquire about golf course architects called "You're Not Playing the Course, You're Playing the Designer." It featured the then unknown Pete Dye, Bob von Hagge, Robert Trent Jones and his sons Rees and Bobby. Apparently the editors liked it because a year later, in 1971, they asked me to write another golf story, this one on the corporate side of Arnold Palmer. Fortunately for me, because my friend John McGrath had worked with Mark McCormack in the branding and selling of Arnie, which is what the story was about. (It was called, "Arnie, Inc.")

Although the story was very favorable to Arnie, Mark and IMG, Palmer was miffed at me for mentioning the part about carousing at Dorado Beach after his victory. "What's Winnie going to think," he groused.

He must have gotten over it, because a year or so later he retained my PR firm to handle his pet project, The Bay Hill Club and Lodge outside Orlando. That was a fun job, and when the PGA Tour brought the Citrus Open to Bay Hill, it blossomed into a popular golf destination.

I particularly recall one day the ad agency for Arnie's clothing line was down getting shots of him on the course to use in their new national campaign. We were standing on the elevated 17th tee, a 207-yard par three over a lake to a green guarded by a long bunker in front.

"Two iron," Arnie said to his longtime caddy. "it's a three-iron," the caddy told him, handing him the three. Palmer frowned but took the three-iron, teed it up while the cameras rolled, the promptly hit it three feet short of the green, the ball trickling back down into the lake.

Now hot, Arnie gave the caddy a steely glare, stalked over to the bag, jammed the three iron into it, and whipped out the earlier-requested two-iron. He teed it up, took his usual mighty swipe, and hit a soaring draw which bounced once and rolled into the cup. Hole in one. Grinning like a Cheshire cat, he strolled back to the bag and looked at the caddy to see what he would say. "It's still a three-iron," the caddy sulked.

The next few times I saw Arnold were at The Landings at Skid-away Island, where I was doing some consulting and he had designed the first of two golf courses. When he saw me on the practice tee he said to the developer, Harold Beck, "Hell, Harold, they let anybody in here!"

That one I particularly remember because they had a small road leading off to the right from the main road, to the golf clubhouse. I named it "Palmer's Draw," after Arnold's famous proclivity for hitting everything right to left.

(In fact, I named The Landings, as well, based on the tale of an early group of Jesuit priests who came ashore on the island and settled there.)

I saw Palmer a few more times at golf seminars I put on for the Urban Land Institute, but the one occasion I remember best was at the opening of his new golf course at The Plantation at Ponte Vedra, near Sawgrass, which had also been a client. As my firm was respon-sible for the opening, we had arranged for Arnold to compete with members on a short par three over water, which he did, lofting a seven iron to within three feet of the flag. Following several flutes of congratulatory champagne, he was then supposed to man a small bull-dozer and carve out some earth for the "groundbreaking" of a new subdivision.

To appreciate this story you have to realize the developer was positioning his golf community as being at one with nature – an early "green" community. Arnold hopped onto the 'dozer, cranked it up, lifted the blade and promptly smashed it into a small pine tree, which toppled over as if whacked by an axe. In Vino Veritas.

Arnie Couldn't Get In!

I was called in to help at The Vintage Club in Indian Wells, California, in early 1981 when the owner had "hit the wall" in sales. After he opened the tony $27 million clubhouse and two Tom Fazio golf courses, real estate and membership sales boomed for about a year.

Most of these sales were from people who were on the waiting list to join Thunderbird and the other exclusive clubs in Palm Springs – and so were ready to become some of the first members of the newly opened Vintage Club.

Shortly after I got there, owner Mick Humphreys held his annual golf tournament, The Vintage Invitational, an event with a blue-chip field which included Arnold Palmer. The first story I heard was that Arnie and a couple of friends had come early to practice before the tournament. He drove his rental car up to the gatehouse, stopped and said "Hi" to the guard. Recognizing him, the guard said "Good morning, Mr. Palmer. Do you have an appointment? Palmer thought he was joking, and said no, he had not. The guard then said "Sorry sir, you'll have to make a U turn here and leave. If you would call the Sales Office they would be happy to make an appointment for you to come in."

SCREECH went the tires on Arnie's rental car as he whipped around the gate house and out onto the street. He was hot. Now fast

David interviewing Dominican President Joaquin Balaguer and Casa de Campo developer Alvaro Carta for an article in the American Airlines inflight magazine.

David goes over script with Jack for a film they made for the PGA of America.

forward to a few years later when Palmer was opening his posh new golf community in Orlando, Isleworth. "By God nobody's getting in here without an appointment, just like the Vintage Club," he told his partners.

I guess that principle must have worked, because he attracted Tiger Woods, Mark McCormack and a bunch of other golf celebrities to become residents.

Jack Nicklaus – Palmer's polar opposite

I don't care how many times they've had their picture taken with arms around each other's shoulders or how wide their smiles, these two guys don't really like each other. Arnie has never really gotten over that first playoff with Jack in the 1962 U. S. Open at Oakmont, where the young blond guy from Ohio putted lights out. When I asked Arnie about it while writing the Esquire piece, he said, "next question."

I first met Nicklaus in 1969 at Lost Tree Village, where he and Barbara and their children lived. As I was doing PR for the tony club community in North Palm Beach, I had gotten the assignment from Golf Digest to write an article about Jack's home life, his family, his fishing and other non-golf interests. During the interviews, he couldn't have been nicer. "Here's my home number," he said, "call me anytime."

We went out to the Gulf Stream on his handsome 41-foot fishing boat, Busy Bee, where Jack fly cast for sailfish and dolphin. During that trip he told me of his lifelong love of fishing, mostly fresh water up till then; and how lucky he felt to be living on the coast in Florida where right offshore was some of the world's finest billfishing.

The story came out in Golf Digest first and then, altered slightly, in The Miami Herald's Sunday Tropic magazine.

Shortly after that Golf Digest published a story I wrote about Pete Dye, titled "Mother Nature, Jack Nicklaus and Me." It was about Dye's new Dominican course, "Teeth of the Dog" at Casa de Campo, a client of mine, and the new Harbour Town track at Sea Pines on Hilton Head Island. Because Jack had hit a few balls on Pete's roughed out fairways during construction, and because Dye's name was not then a household word, the editors put Jack's name in the title. In actuality, Jack showed up on the site a couple of times and has his picture taken with Dye and Charles Fraser, the developer.

That particular article was a great success and spawned others, including Dan Jenkins' famous Sports Illustrated piece on the course.

(Odd fact: One day while going around the not-yet-opened Harbour Town course with Pete Dye and golf writer Charles Price, we came to the 17th hole, a par three along the marsh. There is a sand bunker around the left side of the green, fading back into a long sandy area. Price asked Pete if you could ground your club in the sandy area – clearly not a sand trap. Yes, Pete replied, it isn't a sand trap. "Then what do you call it," Price asked. "I guess you'd call it a waste area," Dye replied. And that's what those non-trap sandy areas have been called ever since.)

Other Nicklaus sightings:

I wrote a script for a short video on golf instruction for the PGA of America. In it were Nicklaus and his long time coach, Jack Grout. We were filming at a club where Grout spent the winter – I believe it was La Gorce on Miami Beach. We printed Jack's script on large white cardboard sheets, and held them behind the camera, and rolled.

The film was about using your club pro to improve your game (which is what Jack did annually with Grout). Jack tried to read it a couple of times, and then said, "I know what to say. Just let me say it without a script." So we did.

"Uhh, the, uh, game....OK, let's go back to the script." So we did, and the video came out fine.

Then there were brief times at events like the PGA Seniors when I was doing PGA National resort; a members and press event with Jack

David, magazine publisher Karl Wickstrom and Jack Nicklaus during interview with Jack for Golf Digest article.

David and golf course architect Pete Dye.

on the 25th anniversary of his course at Sailfish Point; an opening at Ibis in North Palm Beach, and other times. Once or twice Jack would say, "Hi Dave," as we passed in the hall.

To be totally fair to Jack, I must report that something happened to him in his later years. Ten years ago he lost his grandson Jake, a toddler who drowned in a hot tub at Jack's North Palm Beach home.

Since then, Jack and his wife Barbara have been deeply involved in children's charities. They founded the Nicklaus Children's Health Care Foundation and have contributed millions of their own personal wealth, as well as sponsoring and appearing at myriad events. Their contributions to the Miami Children's Hospital have resulted in the facility changing its name to the Nicklaus Children's Hospital.

The Aussies are Awesome

I guess my first Australian player was Bruce Devlin when he began designing golf courses with Robert von Hagge, and was living in Coral Gables. He was a lovely man and joined Bob in recommending me and my firm to his clients.

One day Bruce and his son Kel joined me and my son Chris (boys about 10) on our boat in the Upper Keys. We were nosing around some mangrove islands south of Elliott Key when we reached a little open place where the water was crystal clear.

It looked like there was something moving in the water, so Chris, Kel and I slipped in with our masks and fins. There we encountered an amazing sight: a large school of snook, stacked up like cordwood, milling around and feasting on minnows. "Come look at this, Bruce, "I yelled. "You won't believe your eyes." In he came, and sure enough back in the boat he said, "You're right. I don't believe what I just saw."

Al Barkow, then the editor of Golf Magazine, agreed for me to write a piece on Bruce's design work. I wanted to show that designing golf courses had had an appreciable effect on Bruce's game. So I followed Bruce around a few tournaments, including the World Cup in Palm Beach Gardens. In the article I asserted, as did Bruce, that designing courses with von Hagge had helped him understand design strategy better – what the architect had in mind when he built the course.

Barkow bought the story, although he entertained some doubts about my thesis, and the issue with the article came out during the Hartford Open. Can you imagine my glee when Devlin came strolling down the 18th fairway at Hartford, an easy winner of a tough PGA event? I never found out what Barkow thought, because shortly after that he left the magazine.

Australian tennis players were just as nice and approachable as Devlin. When Gulf + Western built a new tennis center at Casa de Campo in the Dominican Republic to go along with Dye's new golf courses, agents Donald Dell and Ray Benton sold them on hiring Wimbledon star Tony Roche to be their celebrity tennis pro. So Tony promptly invited Harry Hopman's Davis Cup team to visit on their way to their matches in Europe.

Fred Stolle and Ross Case headed up the team, and the boys played several exhibition matches to the delight of the resort's guests.

One day Tony Roche visited me in Miami for some interviews, and agreed to hit a few balls with members at my tennis club in South Miami, Coral Oaks. There was at the time a "white attire only" rule there, but Tony was wearing a bright red Casa de Campo logo shirt that day. He of course was gracious and impressed everyone with his charm and skills with a racquet.

The next day I showed up at Coral Oaks in a yellow shirt. When the pro, Leo Fullwood, saw me, he said, "Hey Pearson, you got to wear white!" I reminded him that Tony Roche had just played yesterday with a red shirt, and he hadn't said anything. "Yeah but you aren't Tony Roche!" he said.

David and Australian tennis star Tony Roche at Casa de Campo.

The serve

On another occasion Newport Beach tennis pro Jacques Grigry brought Roy Emerson, Alex Olmedo and Whitney Reed down to Casa de Campo for a few days' tennis and fishing. Emerson, of course, still holds the record for having won the most tournaments ever. What most people don't know is how funny he is.

Reed (former U. S. Boy's Champion) and I were playing doubles against Emerson and one of the hotel guests. When Emerson hit a forehand to me, the ball would hit the top of the net, trickle over, and plop in my court. After he had done this about three times I realized he was doing it on purpose: his topspin forehand was so accurate he could actually aim for the tape at the top of the net and hit it.

I got to meet several more tennis stars when I was able to bring in Al Bunis' Tennis Grand Masters events to my clients' resorts. We had Rod Laver, Ken Rosewall, Pancho Gonzalez, Gardner Mulloy, Torben Ulrich, Sven Davidson and others at these events. Guests loved them, as the players were gracious at the cocktail parties, and friendly during the guest clinics and exhibitions.

(Small world department: Alvin Bunis, Jr. who was a gifted player growing up, is now the pastor of Plymouth Church in Coconut Grove, where my wife Anne is a member.)

Cliff Drysdale

Fred Stolle introduced me to Cliff Drysdale, the South African Davis Cup star, when we were looking for someone to replace the aging Gardner Mulloy as Director of Tennis at Fisher Island. Drysdale designed an expanded racquet club offering clay, hard and grass surfaces. To keep the ball from hitting the screen and bouncing back on the court, Cliff devised a scheme using cotton netting on the sides instead of wire fencing – hidden from view by a gorgeous hedge of flaming hibiscus.

A year or two after Cliff had re-designed Fisher Island's tennis complex, we were able to bring him up to meet our client at Landfall, an outstanding golf club community outside of Wilmington, North Carolina. As he had at Fisher Island, he developed a racquet club with the cotton netting hidden by flowering bushes, and stayed on as Director of Tennis.

After he had moved into network television as a tennis commentator, Drysdale moved to Key Biscayne, where he designed a superb racquet club for Woody Weiser's Ritz-Carlton Resort and Residences. It was there that he discovered young Australian pro Don Henderson, who became the number one man in their new venture, Cliff Drysdale Tennis Centers.

The two (and a considerable staff of talented young pros) now have Centers all over the U. S. and Canada. (Incidentally, Drysdale held the ranking of Number One World Senior until recently).

Ivan Lendl and the Pepsi Grand Slam

During the 70's and 80's my major client was Arvida (since sold to Disney) Corporation, whose popular club communities covered Florida.

The man developing it was a very bright Californian named Roger Hall. Realizing that Boca West's twin Desmond Muirhead courses would attract only golfers, he built 12 clay tennis courts to attract a wider market. In order to get attention to the tennis, he became the host of a popular TV event called the Pepsi Grand Slam of Tennis. It featured stars like Chris Evert and Marina Navratilova, Jimmy Connors and Vitas Gerulitis.

When Ivan Lendl and Hana Mandlikova came down to play, they fell in love with Boca West and each bought a Hammocks Villa and joined the club. We worked out a discounted price for them in return for a certain number of promotional days a year.

Cliff Drysdale in his heyday as a South African Davis Cup champion.

Incidentally, Arvida Chairman Chuck Cobb and former U. S. Davis Cup star Butch Buchholz took the Pepsi Grand Slam to Key Biscayne, in Miami, and turned it into what became the fifth major – the Lipton. Since then the event has gone through several sponsors, and is now owned by IMG (originally founded by Mark McCormack) and called The Miami Open. There was a huge brouhaha about building the tennis stadium on Key Biscayne property originally donated to the county by the Matheson family. I was consulting for Buchholz at the time, and we were able to work out a compromise that allowed the stadium to be built.

As this is written, the issue has arisen again, with IMG asking to build permanent entertainment structures on the site, and the Matheson family strenuously objecting. So far, the Mathesons seem to be winning.

We opened Pete Dye's acclaimed golf course at Sawgrass, headquarters of the PGA Tour. The annual Tournament Players Championship was played right after the course opened, and it's Dye-like difficult design characteristics gave it instant notoriety in the world of golf.

Over on the West Coast we did the PR for Arvida's Longboat Key Club, which had two golf courses and an outstanding tennis center, as well as a long stretch of sugary white sand. We had established a close working relationship with Al Bunis, who brought his Tennis Grand Masters' finals here. What a thrill it was to meet Rod Laver and Ken Rosewall – both typical down-to-earth Aussies who called you "mate" after knowing you five minutes.

Also in our 17-year run with Arvida were the Boca Raton Hotel and Club, Broken Sound Golf and Racquet Club, and Palm Beach Polo and Country Club.

A Blip on the Screen

Oops, I forgot to mention one blip during that time, which might serve as a warning to young people going into the PR profession. About the time we were doing Sawgrass with Arvida, Jack Healan, the president of Amelia Island Plantation, called us in to help jump-start his new Inn and Tom Fazio golf course.

Having Amelia Island, only an island away from Ponte Vedra, where Sawgrass was located, made it very convenient for me to fly to Jacksonville, rent a car, drive north to Amelia Island, do my work there; and then head south along A1A, take the ferry at Mayport, and drive down to Sawgrass.

One day I got a call from Rick Miller, who headed up Arvida's Florida resorts. "How about meeting me for lunch at the Boca West Club," he asked. When I got there he was seated at a table with co-Arvida executives Roger Hall and Bob Speicher. "Dave," Rick said, "you seem to be representing a competitor of ours, only a few miles away. You are doing Amelia Island, and Sawgrass has the same amenities, similar products, and almost exactly the same market."

I gulped and floundered around trying to find some big differences. "They do?" I asked disingenuously. "I thought Amelia was more of a resort and Sawgrass a private club."

Rick's answer to that was "The answer is simple. Either give up Amelia or all of your Arvida communities." Goodbye Amelia.

Bob Graham and His Workdays

When we moved back to Miami in 1966 to handle Laurance Rockefeller's Caribbean properties, I wrote the article (shown earlier) about the night of November 22, 1963 in the White House – the night of John F. Kennedy's assassination. The article was picked up by the wires and ran all over the country as well as around the world.

As a result of that article, Larry King, who was then doing a late-night radio interview show in Miami, had me on his show twice to discuss the article and my activities in Washington. One of the listeners was a young member of the Florida Senate, Bob Graham – then known as D. Robert Graham.

Graham called and asked if I would be willing to meet with him and his brother Bill at their office in Miami Lakes, the "new town" the Graham family had developed west of Miami. (Incidentally, Bill and Bob Graham were half brothers of Phil Graham, former publisher of the Washington Post, who had been a close friend of JFK's).

When I got there I learned that Bob wanted to run for Governor of Florida. His brother Bill was dubious about the wisdom of his running – and so was I. At the time, Bob was one of Tallahassee's "Dog-house Democrats," so-called by the ultra conservative politicians from North Florida because of Graham and his colleagues' push for progressive environmental legislation.

I told the Grahams that just because I had been in the Kennedy and Johnson Administrations in Washington was not a reason to believe I had any special talent in politics. Nonetheless, they asked me to join their little group speculating about Bob's gubernatorial chances.

The first thing I suggested was that D. Robert Graham become Bob Graham. His name was symbolic of the image he held in the minds of Floridians (that is, those few in South Florida who even knew who he was): he was a Harvard-educated millionaire land developer whose whole career had been spent in the Florida legislature. "We have to change that image if you're going to have any chance," Bill and I told him.

He not only became Bob Graham; he became Bob Graham, man of the people, due almost entirely because of a brilliant idea he conceived of working at 100 different jobs during the campaign. He said it was in order to find out what the people of Florida really wanted, as well as to learn all those jobs. He worked a full shift – in many cases eight hours – for every job.

Bob Squier, the Democratic political media genius, shot Graham at each one of these jobs and ran the spots on television all over the state. Graham sponge diving. Graham serving the homeless. Graham teaching fourth grade. Graham toting garbage cans. He beat all comers and became Governor of Florida in 1978. He served eight years.

During his tenure I conducted a statewide energy conservation campaign called, "Save it, Florida," which was tied to President Carter's new fuel saving initiative. The program was a great success: we made more than one billion impressions with our public service campaign, and energy consumption in the state went down.

One night Jimmy Buffett gave a concert in Tallahassee, and Governor Bob Graham took his teenage daughter Kendall. Buffett's ribald lyrics, of course, were well known to everyone except, apparently, Bob Graham, who musical tastes ran more toward Rodgers and Hammerstein. One number particularly popular with the FSU student body was called "Why Don't We Get Drunk and Screw." Jimmy was to tell me later that when he walked out of his backstage dressing room and saw the Governor there with his teenage daughter, he almost fainted with embarrassment.

It must not have fazed Graham, however, because he asked Buffett if he would lead a statewide campaign to preserve the endangered manatee—a freshwater mammal Jimmy featured in one of his maritime songs ("...sometimes I see me as an old manatee, heading south as the water grows colder...")

Buffett agreed and naturally, Bob Graham called a couple of his default supporters to help form the Save the Manatee Committee: David Pearson and Miami attorney Ron Book.

David advising Florida Governor Bob Graham in his first campaign for the U. S. Senate.

David introducing new Jimmy Buffett public service TV spots, with Buffett and Florida Governor Bob Graham.

Jimmy Buffett feeding cabbage to a baby manatee.

Knowing television stations had a required number of minutes to provide public service time, we prevailed on Buffett to record a series of 30-second TV spots. We got a video production company to produce several PSAs, which became a Pearson/Buffett enterprise: I wrote the scripts, and we used our family's 17-foot Mako with my two daughters Kate and Maggie aboard. Son Chris was at the wheel, speeding down the Intracoastal past, "SLOW DOWN FOR THE MANATEES:" sign. Pointing to the boat, Buffett said "...that's just want I'm talking about, speeding through this manatee zone..."

The campaign worked pretty well; before long the Save the Manatee Club had several chapters and hundreds of members statewide. The endangered mammal's numbers have been stable for some time. Since then, Jimmy's concerts, records and Margaritaville bars and resorts have made him rich enough to move from Key West To Palm Beach, not to mention take up the game of golf.

Other Florida Governors

Of course the first Florida governor I worked for was Le Roy Collins, after he had left the Governor's chair. In working on Bob Graham's campaigns for Governor in 1968 and 1972, I had a chance to get to know his predecessor, Reuben Askew, and his amenuensis, Jim Baccus. Later both of them became law partners.

When Graham was elected Governor, I wrote a few speeches for him. So when Askew announced his run for the Presidency, Jim Baccus asked me if I would write a campaign speech for him, which I did. The final Florida Governor I wrote for was Lawton Chiles, who left his position as U. S. Senator to run for governor "because you can get a lot more done in that job than you can in Washington," he explained.

I wrote Chiles' campaign stump speech when he ran against a Republican incumbent, Governor Bob Martinez. I'll never forget the day I was interviewing him for the speech. He was sitting in the front seat of a State Trooper's car, and I was in the back with a legal pad. After he answered an hour of my questions on his positions, I asked him, "Senator, Florida is still rated 48th in the nation for per capita spending on children's education. We both know that a lot more money is needed for schools. If you're elected, will you propose that we have a state income tax?

There was a pause, and Chiles slowly turned around in his seat to face me. "Not on my watch, my boy."

In more recent times, and as he is currently running for President as I write this, I will mention doing some things with Jeb Bush. Before he ran for Governor of Florida, he was a partner of Armando Codina in the development of Deering Bay, a quiet Bayfront golf and tennis community just south of Miami.

It was decided that Jeb would be the public face of the development, so it was up to me to take him to New York to meet national editors. He was most articulate and winning, and the project gained considerable exposure as a result.

Perhaps the most noteworthy thing that Bush and Codina did in developing Deering Bay was to insist on leaving the mangroves surrounding the golf course untouched. As a result, in 1991 when Hurricane Andrew swept through Miami, the mangroves kept the salt water from ruining the greens and fairways of the course. This and other conservation practices gave the community a sterling reputation in the environmental community.

Golf Course Design, the Saving Grace

My father was a seven handicap golfer who shot in the high '70s, but I never mastered the sweet rhythm he had, and at my best while living at

Sea Pines I was a 10. While working there in the early days, I got to know George Cobb, the architect who designed the first two golf courses. As golf was our major amenity other than the miles of beaches, I found myself learning and writing about golf course architecture.

Through the ensuing years as I specialized in resort and club communities, I found myself getting to know a number of talented and colourful course designers, who became subjects of many free lance magazine and newspaper articles I wrote while trying to generate clients.

There were the aforementioned Jack Nicklaus, Pete Dye, Desmond Muirhead, Robert von Hagge, Tom Fazio and others.

Promoting their names and work along with the client's destination put me in a very desirable position for referrals. And as these celebrity architects were frequently asked by the client who they would use for PR and marketing, they would recommend me. This was especially true of Pete Dye (Casa de Campo, Harbour Town, John's Island etc.), Desmond Muirhead (Haystack, Boca West, Baymeadows, Aberdeen etc.) and Tom Fazio (The Virginian, Moss Creek Plantation, Jupiter Hills, etc.).

From I-95 Fairways to Postage Stamp Greens

When Pete Dye first saw Robert Trent Jones, Sr.'s Palmetto Dunes course on Hilton Head Island, he told Sea Pines developer Charles Fraser "I'm not going to build any of those I-95 fairways at Harbour Town." And indeed he and his consulting partner, Jack Nicklaus, didn't. The nifty little 6,600-yard Harbour Town Golf Links offered golfers just the opposite: narrow fairways along which he left sprawling live oaks whose branches could reach out to stop anything but a very straight drive. And doglegs – sometimes double doglegs – begging to be "cut off," and promising disaster for balls that didn't quite make the corner.

Approaching Dye's greens, golfers found themselves staring at a crazy quilt of greenside sand bunkers, sometimes shored up with two-by-four cypress planks guaranteed to produce prodigious bounces for approaches a few feet short of the green.

He rimmed some greens with creosoted railroad ties, and planted deep pot bunkers *behind* some of his greens. Take that, Tarzan.

Speaking of greens, Harbour Town's were called "postage stamps" by the first group of PGA touring pros who ever played the course. Its inaugural event in 1969, called The Heritage Classic, was won by Arnold Palmer with a score of one under par. The pros' screams could be heard 45 miles away in Savannah.

Dye's instant fame at Harbour Town was assured the following year with the opening of The Teeth of the Dog seaside course at Casa de Campo in the Dominican Republic.

Although I was present at the first Heritage, writing my second Esquire golf article at the time (coincidentally about Palmer), I wasn't working for Sea Pines.

But I was working for the developers of Casa de Campo, a group of Cuban emigres led by a former sugar grower named Alvaro Carta. Carta heard about Pete Dye from the Ecclestone family, who were using him to do their first course at John's Island in Vero Beach. When Carta, who had no experience developing resorts or golf courses, asked Dye who he would recommend to do the promotion of the new resort, Dye said "David Pearson." I'm sure it was because of the Golf Digest article I'd written about him entitled "Mother Nature, Jack Nicklaus and Me." As nobody had ever heard of Pete Dye when I wrote the article, the editors insisted in putting Jack's name in the title, based on his consulting with Pete on the Harbour Town course.

As it turned out, I worked on Casa de Campo for eight years, helping put the first of many future Dominican resorts on the world vacation map. During that time the Minister of Tourism, Victor Cabral, retained my firm to introduce the country in the U. S.

Visionary resort developer Jack Marshall, Pete Dye and David talking over Dye's design of the Old Quarry golf course at Santa Barbara Plantation in Curacao.

I must admit it did help to have Oscar de la Renta build a vacation home on Dye's 14th fairway. With Oscar designing the fashions, we were able to attract Sports Illustrated's bathing suit issue, the first of many national articles about Casa de Campo.

Course Designers and National Magazines

Back to the first major piece I wrote, a six-page article in Esquire, "Six golf architects comment on the aesthetics of the game." The six included British architect Desmond Muirhead, Pete Dye, Robert Trent Jones and Robert von Hagge. Trent Jones, as he was called by his friends, said the three major goals in designing a course were beauty, challenge, and flexibility.

For those not familiar with the many strategies of course design, there are a number that offer golfers alternative routes from tee to green. The most famous is the par five option, in which the designer lays out the hole in such a way that offers the golfer a relatively easy route to the green in three shots (drive, layup fairway wood, short iron into the green), or the chance to "go for it," (drive and a second long wood into the green). The second option, of course, offers the player the chance for eagle, two under par.

Trent Jones famous aphorism was, "Every hole should be an easy bogie and a hard par."

Von Hagge used to characterize design elements such as dog legs, trees, sand trips and bunkers as "descriptive signals," around and through which he routed the hole. His theory was that these "signals" advised the player of trouble, and warned him away. Hence you will usually find some kind of a hazard at every turning point on his fairways.

Although the "classic" designers such as George Fazio and his nephew Tom, Art Hills, Tom Doak, Ben Crenshaw and Bill Coore, who say they create courses based on the "lay of the land," – Jupiter Hills, Champion Hills, Kapalua, The Landings and Bandon Dunes being examples – today's stars, ironically, have reached back to the early architects like Allister MacKenzie and Donald Ross to create a natural, authentic look.

Maybe the latest in this cadre of traditionalists is Gil Hanse, who along with LPGA Hall of Famer Amy Alcott, is designing the new Olympic course in Rio de Janiero.

In between, architects whose work might be called "strategic pragmatic," are designers like Jones' two talented sons, Robert Trent Jones II (Bobby), and Rees Jones, definitely apples who didn't fall far from the tree. Their expansive, imaginative pallets were inherited from their father, called "The Course Doctor," for his work in preparing courses where majors are being played. (For the record, Rees has inherited the title and the assignments).

Perhaps the quintessential neo-classical designer today is David McLay Kidd, a young Scot whose Bandon Dunes and Huntsman Springs tracks put one in mind of the Scottish coastal dunelands. He has also won about every award in the book with these two magnificent layouts.

In the metaphoric realm of apples and trees, you have the uncle/nephew team of George and Tom Fazio (not to mention cousin Jim); father and sons Jack, Jackie and Gary Nicklaus; Pete (and wife Alice) and sons P. B. and Perry Dye, the aforementioned Jones boys; Davis Love and son Davis IV.

Other designers I have worked with include Gary Player, Jay Morrish, Bruce Devlin, Ben Crenshaw, Bill Coore, and Bobby Weed.

Pete, Alice, and P. B. Dye et al

Following that Esquire piece in 1971, much of my PR business came out of referrals by the golf architects. The fact is that in the early days

From left, Golf architects George Fazio and his nephew Tom Fazio describe their new golf course at Moss Creek Plantation.

Co-designers Gil Hanse and Amy Alcott at the site of their new Olympic golf course in Rio.

David interviews former touring star and golf designer Tom Weiskopf, designer of Pearson client Old Kinderhook golf course in Missouri.

of my firm, to supplement my income from my few clients, I did a lot of freelance magazine writing and developed some knowledge of the craft.

And since I was working with designers like the Dyes, Jack Nicklaus, Arnold Palmer, Bob von Hagge, Desmond Muirhead, Tom Fazio, George Cobb, Robert Trent Jones and his sons Rees and Bobby, Joe Lee, Art Hills, Bobby Weed, Greg Norman and others, I had found a specialty in writing about golf architecture. My pieces ran in Golf World, Golf Magazine, Golf Digest, Esquire and in all the major in-flight publications.

Later when the editors realized I was including some of my clients' places in the articles, my freelance golf writing days came to an end. But that was ok – I could still write pieces on other subjects – politics, conservation, tennis, travel, real estate – and did to this day. (This memoir being an example).

But the most fun I had in these years was with Dye, who was a rough and ready World War II veteran from Urbana, Ohio. He married a socialite named Alice O'Neill while they were students at Rollins College (Alice went on to become a legendary women's amateur champion), and didn't have to worry about money in the early years as he got started. After my Golf Digest piece about him, Pete referred me to Alvaro Carta, the president of Golf + Western Americas, who owned 10,000 acres in the Dominican Republic which became the storied Casa de Campo resort destination.

Later I worked with his son P. B., who is a character is his own right, on the highly successful Puntacana Resort and Club on the eastern end of Hispanola.

One of my favorite ads of all time was a full page color aerial shot of an oceanfront hole on P. B.'s La Cana course, whose green was fronted by a menacing series of church-pew bunkers, with snowy sand and translucent turquoise ocean behind. The headline said:

"DON'T BE SHORT"
P. B. Dye
Course Designer

After that I joined the Dyes in working on the new Santa Barbara Plantation in Curacao, where they built their challenging Old Quarry golf course. My favourite ad there had the headline:

"6,000 YEARS AGO THE ARAWAKS CAME TO CURACAO.
THEN THE SPANISH.
THEN THE DUTCH.
THEN PETE DYE.

Obviously I was having a lot of fun writing ads for the Dyes.

Wildman Bob von Hagge and the White Witch

Bob von Hagge had never forgotten me since he was one of the six golf architects I featured in my big Esquire golf design story in the early '70s. He recommended us for as many resorts as he could.

There are almost too many hilarious incidents with von Hagge to single out one. He was a tall Viking of a guy, blond hair and light blue eyes, who learned the business under the famous Dick Wilson. Among his penchants was naming golf courses after the characteristics he had built into them. The White Witch, at Rose Hall in Jamaica ("Her gentle slopes will seduce you until you turn a dogleg and she whips you with a fierce wind from the east."). The Gold Course at Doral ("I call it the Bitch Goddess.")

Once while driving to meet with a delegation of native Americans from the Jicarilla Apache Tribe in New Mexico, Bob cautioned us about one of the Indians. "Don't look at his earlobes," he warned us. "He has

6,000 years ago the Arawaks came to Curaçao.
Then the Spanish. Then the Dutch.

Then Pete Dye.

Santa Barbara Plantation.
Unquestionably the finest golf and marina resort community in the Caribbean.

Fifteen hundred acres of oceanfront, bayfront, hillside and fairway residences set in the splendor of Spanish Water bay. Offshore, colorful reefs below crystal-clear waters. Onshore, the new Hyatt Regency Curaçao Golf Resort, Spa and Marina, Pete Dye's *Old Quarry* Golf Course, Peter Burwash International Tennis Center and the 120-slip Seru Boca Marina. Nearby, the fascinating Dutch Colonial town of Willemstad, free-port shopping and museums.

For real estate information call 305.661.2009 or visit www.santabarbaraplantation.com

A great example of promoting the golf course architect while promoting the resort.

The signature hole at von Hagge's spectacular White Witch golf course at Rose Hall, Jamaica.

these pendulous earlobes that look like they have a couple of Titleists in them." Of course all of us gazed straight at the guy's earlobes when we met him. (P. S. We didn't get the job).

Von Hagge did come through for us in several big ways, however; not the least of which was his recommendation to billionaire John Rollins that he retain us to promote his new golf and beach resort outside of Montego Bay, Jamaica. Called Rose Hall after the eponymous 18th Century sugar plantation estate house overlooking the Caribbean, the development featured two von Hagge golf courses, a luxurious Ritz-Carlton hotel, and a community of stunning vacation homes.

Although his "White Witch" course got most of the publicity because of its dramatic contours and name, the reality is that the better design of the two is actually Cinnamon Hill.

(Brief note on Cinnamon Hill: when von Hagge built it, he named it Three Palms after the three palm trees marking the graves of Annie Hall's three lovers, according to the legend. Annie, called the White Witch by her slaves, was the owner of Rose Hall Plantation.

According to the story still being told since her death in 1837, she had each of her three husbands garrotted by a slave, and then had the slave murdered as well. She was supposed to have buried each under a palm tree. Thus when we were designing the logo for the new golf course, I was trying to find the three palm trees. I asked the greens superintendent where they were located. "Where do you want them?" was his reply.)

In addition to a number of still-standing sugar plantation ruins and overseers' tombstones, country and western superstar Johnny Cash and his wife June Carter Cash had a house on a fairway built in the late 1800's by the family of Elizabeth Barrett Browning. The house was called Cinnamon Hill, after which the course was subsequently named.

We opened the Ritz-Carlton and the White Witch with a series of events that got national attention. First was the hotel opening featuring a new video we made of Johnny and June Carter Cash. They had written a song about Annie Palmer and her ill-fated husbands, which we premiered that night.

Next was an international boy's golf tournament with young players from around the world – accompanied of course by golf writers from each country. Finally, we filmed Shell's Wonderful World of Golf, pitting the young Apache Indian Notah Begay II against veteran PGA Tour star Hal Sutton. This telecast, along with stories by a number of top golf and travel writers, put Rose Hall and the White Witch on the international map.

Bruce Devlin, Architect and Touring Pro

Von Hagge had adopted Australian touring pro Bruce Devlin as his co-designer, and asked me to help Bruce gain some attention in his new role. After following him around the course at a World Cup event in Palm Beach, it occurred to me that in laying out golf courses, he would gain insights into what the architect had in mind in designing the course – and that he could put that knowledge to work in improving his own game.

I asked him if this was true, and he averred that it definitely was. "Since I started working with Bob von Hagge," he said, "I have gained tremendous insight into the different strategies hidden in each course – and how this insight can help the golfer in playing that course."

Ironically, the month my article on Devlin came out in Golf Magazine he won the Hartford Open, thus validating my theory of his design work improving his golf game. (Several years later while playing tennis with Golf editor Al Barkow in Miami, I reminded him of Devlin winning the Hartford. "You caught a break, Pearson," Barkow said, "because the following week he was lucky to make the cut.")

David, 1976

David, 1985. (Note pre-computer Olympic manual typewriter)

Desmond Muirhead. Burly, Bearded Briton

Most of the golf course designers were offbeat – a few you might even call eccentric. Muirhead was a Cambridge-educated Scot who designed symbols into his courses. One course, Aberdeen in Florida, had a "Marilyn Monroe" hole, complete with shapely breasts which guarded a face framed with powdery bunkers. Pete Dye looked at the course one day and said, "That's one course you have to play from a helicopter."

Muirhead's non-traditional golf holes were often shaped in the form of a goddess or an animal. At Stone Harbor, New Jersey, the green on one par three looks like Medusa; and another is shaped like a crouching tiger. As a planner, he relied heavily upon carefully supervised construction techniques while the course was being built. His courses tend to be expansive, with limited roughs and wide, sculptured greens.

Desmond's career went up and down. Starting out in Hawaii as a land planner on the massive Kaiser Plantation where he designed his first course, he located in Newport Beach, California and there began to build some of the most innovative and unusual courses in America.

When Arvida Corporation's young executive team was recruited in California and imported to Florida, they brought Muirhead with them to design the first two courses at their major Boca West development in Palm Beach County. This was in the early '70s when I had just moved from Atlanta to Miami and started my PR firm. Arvida became one of my early clients, and Boca West the first of their golf communities I was to promote.

While he was in Florida, Desmond met Jack Nicklaus, who lived only a few miles up the coast from Boca Raton in North Palm Beach. Nicklaus had learned a little from having worked with Pete Dye on Harbour Town, but he realized he needed more professional training, and so he brought Desmond aboard to co-design several courses. Among them were New St. Andrews in Japan, Muirfield Village in

Ohio, and Myakoo Lakes in Palm Beach County.

Here's where I come in again. One day I was playing tennis at my neighbourhood club in Miami with a friend, John Underwood, who was a senior writer at Sports Illustrated. He said to me, aren't you a friend of Desmond Muirhead's? I said I was, and he then told me that he was writing a major piece on Nicklaus and his new golf design career. He said he had interviewed Jack and Desmond on several occasions and that Desmond was in the story. Then, he said, one night Jack called him and said "Take Muirhead out of the story – he's no longer with me."

The problem, Underwood said, was "that although the editors had deleted the references to Muirhead in my piece, it was too late to re-move a picture of Jack and Desmond looking at a set of plans in Japan. Shortly after the magazine story came out, I got a call at 3 am from London." It was Desmond calling. "That bloody bastard!" he yelled. "He's cut me out of the story but left my picture in, with no caption!" Sic Semper Tyrannus.

Joe DiMaggio, George Bush, etc.

One day I got a call from my client, Jeb Bush and Armando Codina's Deering Bay Golf Club and Marina, a posh condo community on Bis-cayne Bay with an Arnold Palmer golf course, racquet club and ma-rina. The caller, Ken Rosen, was one of the developers of the community. He said they were signing a contract with Joe DiMaggio wherein Deering Bay would provide DiMaggio a luxurious two bed-room condo, rent free, in return for six days a year of his time pro-moting the community.

I was given the assignment of filling the six days of DiMaggio's time with events and interviews that would tie the Yankee Clipper to the development.

A couple of these days were notable. Deering Bay's developer Ar-mando Codina and his partner Jeb Bush invited Jeb's father, former

President George Bush, and DiMaggio to play an exhibition round on the course Arnold Palmer had designed.

Although the event was staged for club members, residents and their guests only, a crowd of several hundred gathered around the first tee to watch these notables. As each was saying a few words to the crowd, I noticed that Joe had a frown on his face. Hmm, I thought. On a hunch, I sidled up next to him and whispered, Joe, would you like to take a short bathroom break? Would I! he said. So we slipped through the crowd to the empty locker room.

When he emerged, he had a wide smile on his face and a springier step to the first tee.

(Incidentally, DiMaggio teed off with a low-flying hook straight down the middle of the first fairway, a double in anybody's league.)

My next encounter with the Yankee Clipper was the most interesting of all. Realizing that few people in Miami knew DiMaggio was living at Deering Bay, I invited Herald sports columnist Bob Rubin to interview him in his spacious condo.

After he graciously offered us coffee and juice, we sat down in the living room with Joe and his business manager Morris Engelberg, a Ft. Lauderdale attorney. Di Maggio's gatekeeper would be too mild a word for him: Nothing happened with Joe that didn't go through Engelberg. The ground rules were laid: no questions about Marilyn Monroe, only questions about baseball and life at Deering Bay.

The first thing Bob Rubin asked him was something every baseball fan would like to know: "Joe, how did your 56-game hitting streak end?" A wide smile creased DiMaggio's face as he told the story of that fateful July day in Cleveland, where the Yankees faced the Indians. On the first game of the series, Joe had three hits.

The next night, it went like this: first at-bat, he pulled a low curveball over the third base bag which Ken Keltner backhanded and threw him out at first. Second at-bat, he walked. In the seventh, Keltner, remembering DiMaggio's his earlier pulled drive, edged a couple of steps closer to the bag.

DiMaggio hit a rifle shot over the third base bag. Keltner made a backhanded stab that propelled him into foul territory, but his long throw beat Joe to first by a step. In the eighth, DiMaggio grounded into a double play, and his streak was over.

"Next day I got two hits which started a 16-game streak. If Keltner hadn't moved out of his normal position, that drive would have been a double," he said quietly, shaking his head at the memory.

Ted Williams' Tennis Temper

The same sportswriter, John Underwood, referred to above, wrote the bestseller "My Turn at Bat" with the legendary Ted Williams. Bonding through that book, they became friends are did several more together over the years. Williams, a fishing aficionado, had a winter home in Islamorada in the Florida Keys.

One day I got a call from John asking if I'd like to join him and play tennis with Ted Williams, who was visiting on his way to the Keys. I drove over to Coral Oaks Tennis Club in South Miami, where John and I were both members, and played together regularly.

I was given Williams as a doubles partner, and John played with a neighborhood friend named Ed Woitke.

You would think that Ted Williams would have a fearsome serve and awesome forehand, given the power of his baseball swing. Just the opposite. Playing with his right hand (remember he batted lefty), the Splendid Splinter unveiled an array of junk the likes of which I had rarely ever seen. His stuff made Bobby Riggs look like a piker. "Uh oh John," he would tease when offering a soft drop shot to Underwood when John was way back behind the baseline, "hurry, hurry...you'll never get there."

Oscar de la Renta, who recommended David to the Rainieri family to do the public relations and advertising for Punta Cana Resort & Club.

John Underwood interviewing Ted Williams for "My Turn at Bat."

It was all spin and touch shots, with an occasional dink thrown in when you were expecting a smash. We were all laughing our heads off, and of course Williams and I were winning. Then appeared the old Ted Williams Boston fans knew so well. He hit an overhead long and the ball lodged in the screen about 10 feet up.

"You sonofabitch," he yelled at his racquet, and running over, threw it up to dislodge the ball. When they both came down, he picked up the racquet and whacked it a few times on the ground. "There," he yelled at the poor racquet, "that ought to teach you!" (The other salty remarks he made that day cannot be repeated in this book, which I hope my grandchildren will read.)

(In his latter years when Williams he would call, he would say, "It's only me." So when he died a few years ago, John used that greeting as the title of his memoir of his time with his friend, Teddy Ballgame. In my opinion, it is the best piece of work Underwood ever did – and he wrote some great stories during his Sports Illustrated career.)

Oscar de la Renta

One of my more recent clients was Puntacana Resort and Club in the Dominican Republic, a very successful resort community developed by Frank Rainieri with financial help from labor lawyer Ted Kheel.

I had been experienced in the Dominican when I was doing the PR and marketing for Casa de Campo. Fashion icon Oscar de la Renta had built an attractive seaside home on the Pete Dye golf course overlooking the Caribbean.

We of course used him and his name in the early promotion of Casa de Campo.

When Rainieri built his international airport and first resort hotel at Punta Cana, Oscar went over and was captivated by the endless stretch of palm fringed beaches (unlike Casa de Campo, which had one small man-made beach, Las Minitas). He asked Rainieri if he could invest, and Frank sold him an oceanfront site near his own house in a private section he called Corales.

Rainieri brought Pete's son P. B. Dye over to design an oceanfront golf course, and later, with the success of the resort, imported Tom Fazio to build a seaside layout as well.

Oscar built a lovely Caribbean-style home at Corales, and invited Misha Baryshnikov and Julio Iglesias to do the same. As all three were quite cooperative, we were able to use their names and pictures in a number of ads and of course in publicity.

Other celebs who came to Punta Cana included Bill and Hillary Clinton, who spent every Easter as Oscar's guests.

Recent Days

In more recent times I have been on the Board of Tropical Audubon, working to promote the rehabilitation of The Everglades and to clean up Biscayne Bay. My main raison d'etre has been to encourage my developer clients to plan their projects in a way that would allow for maximum preservation of the habitat – in Florida chiefly pine uplands, marsh and wetlands, as well as the threatened coastal dunelands.

Maybe the proudest I am of my years doing then-Governor Bob Graham's "Save it, Florida" energy conservation campaign, his "Save Our Shoreline" campaign, and his "Save the Manatee" campaign, was being given the Florida Audubon Society's Chairman's Award in 1988.

The plaque states:

> "His creative and innovative talents have promoted the
> goals and objectives of the society for many years and
> who, by donating his time and professional services, has
> made the public more aware of Florida's Environment."

Sarge Never Stopped

One day in 1992 I got a phone call from Sarge Shriver, who, after his tenure as Ambassador to France and his run for the Presidency, had jumped in to help his wife Eunice Kennedy Shriver with the organization she founded, Special Olympics. "Hello Dave," Sarge yelled in his exuberant way, "how the hell are you, basking on those Florida beaches every day?"

It turned out what he wanted was for me to help him found a "Miami Mega-City Special Olympics" program, something he was initiating in big cities around the U. S. Of course there was never any way to say no to Sarge.

So I rounded up about 10 of Miami's business and sports leaders and got my Fisher Island client to host a luncheon for them. Every one of them agreed to serve on his Management Council. Much against my wishes, I was elected Chairman of the Council, where I served for a year.

Another time as I was walking through an airport my cell phone rang and it was Sarge again. "Dave," he said, "I need you to help get some exposure for Maria. She's new on NBC's news team, and she's a great girl who really isn't fully appreciated," he said. I listened, but there really wasn't much I could do to promote his lovely daughter – who didn't need it anyway.

Shortly after that she married movie star strong man Arnold Schwartzneger, who went on to become Governor of California and she, first lady.

The coda to that story is that a few years later Shriver and Eunice were in Miami where he was making a speech honoring Chesterfield Smith, an attorney who had devoted his life to human rights.

At the cocktail party before the speech, my wife Anne and I approached a group talking with Eunice. "Hello Pearsons! she said, calling us through the crowd to her side. "I haven't seen you both for such a long time!" She and Anne then laughed about the first time we met, when she had invited us to Sunday lunch at their Maryland country home. "Do you remember we talked about how to get our kids to drink their milk? Anne asked. "Indeed I do," Eunice answered. "Put in lots of chocolate!"

Eunice asked about our children and Anne told her our son had married a Cuban girl, and one of our daughters an Argentine. "Oh I know what that's like," she laughed. "Our daughter married a Austrian!"

The Interview with Baby Doc

In the summer of 1984, two years before he abdicated his "Presidency for life" and flew to France, Baby Doc Duvalier decided he needed to change Haiti's image from that of a dictatorship to an investment and tourist- friendly island. One day I got a call from a client named Jack Bernstein, co-owner of Miami's Everglades Hotel. A Haitian hotel-owner friend had called asking him who he used for public relations, and would he recommend them to Baby Doc to do the PR for Haiti.

Although I was well aware that Duvalier was indeed a dictator, I had the glimmer of a notion that maybe he was preparing to change his style of governing. It was a long shot, but what the hell. I had been working in Haiti in the late '70s, doing a mountain top casino hotel in Petionville called El Rancho (a hideaway for the then not-married Elizabeth Taylor and Richard Burton). The country was lovely, the people kind and hospitable, and the poverty was overwhelming.

Maybe a new tourism campaign was what was needed. So I flew down to Port Au Prince.

I was met at the airport by Bernstein's friend the hotelier, who took me to his place and checked me in. He told me that the President wanted a few of his close advisors to meet me before my interview with him. So all the next day I was visited by friends of Baby Doc's: mostly young men in expensive suits being chauffer-driven to the hotel.

They would ask what I thought of Haiti, of the President, of their politics – not much about my experience, all about my attitude. Clearly they were checking me out so they could report to Duvalier.

I must have passed muster because that evening I got word that I had an appointment with the President the following morning at the Palace. When I arrived there I was met by a sergeant who led me to the office of the Minister of the Interior. (I later found out he was the equivalent of the CIA – and head of the dreaded Ton Ton Macoutes). He, too, had several questions for me about my attitude about Haiti.

Then he led me down a corridor to Baby Doc's office. We went inside, and the Interior Minister stayed and acted as translator. (Although it became clear to me after a few minutes that Duvalier understood English perfectly well – he was just pretending that he didn't.)

Baby Doc was a pleasant-looking, roundfaced fellow, light brown skin, dressed in a beige leisure suit.

"What do you think of Haiti?" he asked me. I told him I thought it was a lovely country with perhaps the most hospitable people in the Caribbean. "Can you get the New York Times and the Miami Herald to write good stories about us, and stop denigrating me and my government?"

My answer to this, the key question of the interview, was complex. I basically said that the only thing necessary for that to happen was for him to announce he was holding free democratic elections. "But we already have them," he protested. No, I said, not for just the parliament. But for his office – for the Presidency.

"I cannot do that," he said, "because the people have elected me President for Life, the same as my father." And thus went the conversation, with Duvalier unwilling to consider a free election.

"Besides," he continued, the United States should consider us good friends. We are your biggest supporter in the Caribbean. Look at Cuba, a Communist country. The Dominicans elected Juan Bosch, clearly a Socialist. Grenada is a Russian ally. We are the only country the U. S. can depend upon!"

The meeting ended with me telling Duvalier that my firm would represent Haiti on one condition: that he would call for free elections, and allow others to run for the Presidency. I didn't really think he would do that, but who knows.

I was driven to the airport and there met a Mr. Bennett, the father of Baby Doc's wife. He asked me what my expenses were. I told him $1,500 including airfare. He pulled out a personal checkbook and wrote out a check for $1,500 and handed it to me quietly. Then he left.

I caught the plane to Miami, and a month later learned that Haiti had hired a major national firm to do its public relations. There was never a free democratic election from that time until he abdicated in 1986.

Other Colorful Characters in the Play

Anne Stuart Bates Pearson

This wouldn't be a full picture of my career if I didn't mention some of the other people whose paths I crossed, some of whom were not only great fun but also tremendously helpful.

My wife Anne, first of all a very goodlooking lady who has retained the original appeal she had for me and several other guys when we met in 1955, and perhaps the most voracious reader of modern fiction I have ever met, who acts as a "taster" for me. Since she reads three times faster than I do, she advises me as to whether I will like a book or not. No matter how many nights I spend reading her fiction recommendations and the histories and biographies I love, there are still at least 10 books waiting on the living room table.

Anne is from Webster Groves, Missouri, and as such has brought a Mid-Western sensibility (accent on sense) into my life; many times pulling me back from the brink of a decision I would later regret.

Early on we decided to take summer family vacations, and through the years our son Christopher (Chris) and two daughters Margaret (Maggie) and Katherine (Kate) have gone with us to the beach on Hilton Head Island…to London and the Cottswolds…to Paris, Berlin, and in the case Kate, to study in Spain.

Charles Fraser and John McGrath

These two fellows, along with Chuck James, Pete Caudle and Wally Butler, were the original developers of Sea Pines Plantation on Hilton Head Island. Charlie and John had met in Yale Law School, and both were not only brilliant visionaries, but also the best friends a young man could ever have.

When I was working with the national PR firm of Bell & Stanton in Atlanta in 1965, John McGrath, who had joined Laurance Rockefeller's resort development team, asked me to leave the big firm, move to Miami, and start my own. Thus my first client was Laurance Rockefeller, and my job was to promote his resorts at Caneel Bay and Little Dix Bay in the Virgin Islands, and Dorado Beach Hotel in Puerto Rico.

McGrath had also been a partner of Mark McCormack, founder of the worldwide IMG sports network, and while with Mark he handled Arnold Palmer's business affairs. Thus it was that I was introduced to Palmer, and after a few years began handling the PR for his Bay Hill Club in Orlando.

Porter Anderson

I met Porter in my dorm at Emory. As a returning veteran, I was given a number of perks and jobs on campus, including being dorm counselor in return for free rent. Porter and I shared a number of affinities: we were both concerned about Emory's lack of blacks in the student body, we both were aficionados of Mozart, we both played tennis (he good enough to be an alternate on the Emory tennis team), were both southerners, and loved beer and girls.

He was a tall, blond haired, blue eyed Alabamian, quite shy and self-effacing. You would never have guessed he would turn into a world-renowned scientist if you had met him when I did.

Briefly, Porter won a Woodrow Wilson Fellowship to Harvard, where he obtained a Ph.D. in Biochemistry. He went into immunology research, and after a number of years, was the co-discoverer of a vaccine for infant meningitis.

This vaccine was such a breakthrough that he won the Lasker Prize as well as the UNESCO Award. The United Nations estimated that his vaccine had saved the lives of more than 640,000 children – and that was five years ago. Pediatricians all over the world now give the vaccine along with DPT shots to infants.

He is now semi-retired and lives on Biscayne Bay in Miami, where he rows his small dinghy out to a nearby reef and snorkels among the mangrove snappers.

John Underwood and Tom Rainey

I believe I mentioned John in connection with Ted Williams, who was his close friend. and amanuensis. John authored "My Turn at Bat," Ted's first book, followed by "The Science of Hitting," and on his death, "It's Only Me," a tribute to their long friendship and collaboration.

John was a Senior Editor for Sports Illustrated for many years, and is still considered one of the magazine's most talented writers.

He and I played tennis with our mutual friend Tom Rainey, a veterinarian who picked up the game after he saw me playing with John. (After two months of lessons from the club pro, he "came out" and proceeded to beat both of us for the next 20 years).

It seems impossible, but John and Tom have been friends now for 48 years. (I know, how can that be when I'm only 54?)

Frank Carlton

I met Frank during his year off from Emory medical school to study humanities. We took Shakespeare together and had a blast memorizing lines and quizzing each other on our way to A's. His future wife Huldah was one of my tennis phys ed students. Frank's sensitivity to language and literature has been a joy to me from our student days onward.

Frank, who is a world-class angler (bonefish in the Bahamas, salmon in Alaska, tarpon in the Keys) was part of an incredible experience we both had one summer day over Molasses Reef, in the Florida Keys. We were snorkeling there, looking at the colorful reef with its many kinds of tropical fish.

All of a sudden we saw something flashing under the water about 15 yards away from us. As we swam slowly toward the action, it suddenly became clear that it was two full grown sailfish mating. What a sight. Both had their dorsal fins spread out, and the late afternoon sun flashed across their silver sides as they rolled and cavorted before us.

To this day I have never heard of any other swimmer who ever witnessed two sailfish mating in the Florida Keys. Maybe someone has seen them in a tank, but in the open ocean.....

(And as he was the first to read the draft of this memoir, I of course will hold him responsible for any errors of fact or egregious misuse of metaphors herein.)

Bits and Pieces

Dennis Martinez

One day Dennis Martinez walked unannounced into my Coral Gables office. Martinez, called "El Presidente" in his native Nicaragua, was a major league pitching star who began with the Baltimore Orioles in 1976 and ended with the Atlanta Braves in 1998.

He had heard of my work in Mexico and wanted to know if I could put his planned Nicaraguan lakefront resort on the map. Although it looked lovely – a cluster of bamboo cottages along a volcanic mountain lake – he had no funds for the development. I told him that although I would love to work with him, I wasn't into raising capital for development. Pleasant meeting, that was all.

Captain Crunch, Amy Alcott et al

Somehow I developed a local reputation for being good in promoting sports professionals, although truth to tell, I'm not sure how that happened. One day in the late '60's I got a visit from a young Miami Dolphins linebacker named Mike Kolen, who because of his powerful hitting was nicknamed "Captain Crunch." We had some good talks, but nothing really came of it.

A golf tournament called the Women's International was played at one of my clients' courses, Moss Creek Plantation, near Hilton Head Island. While handling the event I met several lady golfers, among them a rising star named Amy Alcott. Later when she was playing an event in Miami she came to visit me in my home, looking for advice on how to promote herself on the LPGA tour. I gave her some tips, but nothing came of it except a long term friendship. Later in her career she was inducted into the LPGA Hall of Fame, and lately I have been helping her develop her golf course design business.

Currently she is co-designing the new Olympic golf course in Rio de Janiero with Gil Hanse.

The Tennis Grand Masters,
Cliff Drysdale and Butch Buchholz

Although golf was the main amenity characterizing most of my clients' resorts, tennis was also a major factor in promoting them.

One of the most successful events we used to trumpet this sport at our resorts was The Tennis Grand Masters, a group of touring former stars put together by a Midwestern entrepreneur named Al Bunis. Bunis was a genial millionaire and an amateur tennis player who came up with the brilliant idea of rousing former world-class players like Pancho Gonzalez, Ken Rosewall and Rod Laver, and putting them into a rollicking group who toured the finer tennis clubs and resorts in the U.S.

We brought Bunis and his players to several of our clients' resorts through the years, including Seabrook Island Club and Resort in Charleston, Longboat Key Club in Sarasota, and Fisher Island Club in Miami Beach.

The format called for the pros to arrive on Friday and attend a welcome party that evening, to which club members and resort guests were invited (with special attention paid to prospective real estate buyers). The old pros were great at meeting and greeting, and the social part of their weekend was probably as important as the actual tennis.

Saturday morning the pros would conduct a clinic for the members, and they would play their first matches in the afternoon. Saturday night was usually an outdoor barbecue or beachside oyster roast, with final matches played Sunday morning.

When we first met Al Bunis his group consisted of players like Gardner Mulloy, Pancho Gonzalez, Vic Seixas, Torben Ullrich and Sven Davidson. After a few years those players were replaced by later stars like Rosewall and Laver, and South African Davis Club star Cliff Drysdale, ranked number one senior player in the world at the time.

After retiring from active competition, Drysdale became a network TV commentator. He and his partner Don Henderson now operate 11 tennis centers throughout the country.

Arvida was able to host the Pepsi Grand Slam of Tennis, a made-for-TV event that brought in such stars as Jimmy Connors, Chris Evert and Martina Navratilova. One year the winners were Ivan Lendl and Hana Mandlikova. And one of the great PR thrills of my life came that Monday morning when the headline of the Sports Section of the New York Times read, "CZECH MATES!"

Fortuitously, Lendl was so happy with Boca West that he went on to buy a Hammocks Villa there, trading a discount on the price for several promotional days a year.

The Children

One daughter who worked with our firm for 15 years, Margaret (Maggie), graduated from Anne's alma mater, Hollins College, and works in development at St. Timothy's school in Baltimore. Katherine (Kate), our youngest, the third generation Pearson to graduate from Emory, earned a Master's at Middlebury followed by a career in documentary films, having started at CNN and segueing through HBO Latin America and the Documentary Channel. She is now with Maryland Public Television. Son Christopher (Chris) also majored in History at the University of Miami, and has been my partner in the public relations firm off and on for 25 years — with time off for his service in the U. S. Army during the Iraqi War. He is currently running a driving school for teenagers.

Still At It At 84

As I write the last words in this memoir, my son Chris and I are working with former Senator Bob Graham and his Florida Conservation Coalition in a major statewide effort to lobby public officials – especially legislators, as they're the ones who allocate, or withhold, funds for restoring the Everglades and other critical efforts to preserve our freshwater resources.

Coda

To any young persons reading this memoir themselves drawn to some aspects of my career, I can only say if the door opens, go in. Give it a try. You'll never know what fun and satisfaction await you if you pass it by.

When I was at Emory I majored in History, as I had no idea of a career, and I wanted to get as broad an education as possible. I did not have a career plan, but took everything as it came. In my philosophy, life proceeds by hazard, accident and chance.

That said, there were a few open doors that I passed by, and I have always wondered, what if….

The teaching assistantship to Indiana that I passed up while indulging my fantasies with girls and rum in Havana…the possibility of going higher up in government when I quit my GS-17 job as Assistant Director of the U. S. Community Relations Service to go back south into unknown territory…If I'd taken the job Bill Bartholomay offered me with the Atlanta Braves and continued a career in the Major Leagues….

But the truth is I don't regret passing those open doors, because just down the way were more opportunities waiting. Including a fascinating career in public relations.

Finally, if there's anything in my career I'm really proud of, it's trying to adhere to the principle I told Sargent Shriver I intended to follow when he kidded me about going from the Peace Corps and Civil Rights to work for the Rockefellers at Caneel Bay. I said "Sarge, I'm going to moonlight for my altruism."

So although I certainly could have made a lot more money spending all my time on business, I wouldn't have been able to say yes to my mother's voice whispering in my ear when those groups came around looking for Pro Bono service, "you know you should help them."

APPENDIX

In looking at my website the other day I counted the number of clients we had served in the 49 years between Laurance Rockefeller in 1966 and Huntsman Village in 2015:

225 clients.

Here are a few of the more interesting aspects of our time with them.

- Lost Tree Village, North Palm Beach – where Jack Nicklaus was living when I wrote the first Golf Digest article about him and his family. As Lost Tree was private, this was about the only way I could get national publicity for them. I was learning a hard lesson.

- Dorado Beach, Puerto Rico – I met some fascinating characters while doing their PR and advertising: Chi Chi Rodriguez was their head golf pro, and Nick Bollettieri was their tennis pro.

- Royal Westmoreland, Barbados – Robert Trent Jones, Jr. (Bobby) recommended us for this one, a British client building a lovely golf community.

- Rose Hall, Jamaica – Robert von Hagge introduced us to the Rollins family, where we opened their new Ritz-Carlton Hotel as well as two great golf courses. We brought in Shell's Wonderful World of Golf, and had Johnny Cash living there as a bonus.

- Vintage Club, Palm Springs – Developed a special marketing campaign for this private club community which helped developer Mick Humphries sell out two years early.

- Palmas del Mar, Puerto Rico – Did this one twice. First in its early days as part of the Charles Fraser empire, and 25 years later in a "Renaissance" program with the opening of a new Rees Jones golf course.

- Santa Barbara Plantation, Curacao – The late Jack Marshall developed this Pete and P. B. Dye golf and marina resort, and remembered us from our days at Vintage Club.

- Casa de Campo, Dominican Republic – We helped put both Pete Dye and his Teeth of the Dog golf course on the map here, where we also met resident Oscar de la Renta. We kept this client for eight years.

- Ministry of Tourism, Dominican Republic – We became known for the success of Casa de Campo, and created a U. S. campaign which opened the country to tourism.

- Punta Cana, D.R. – Both P. B. Dye and Oscar de la Renta recommended us to the Rainieri family to promote this extensive resort. We worked there for seven years.

- Punta Mita, Mexico – We were recommended by EDSA, the international planning firm, to create a major marketing plan for Grupo Ica, developers of this Pacific coast resort.

- Playacar, Mexico – It was Robert von Hagge who once more recommended us to open this golf and beachfront resort in Playa del Carmen, just south of Cancun.

- The Landings of St. Lucia – Once again with Rockresorts, we did the U. S. public relations for this Canadian-owned Caribbean resort community.

- Turks & Caicos Ministry of Tourism – One of our most interesting and beautiful island resort locations, we handled their national public relations for two years.

- Consejo Nacional de Turismo, Mexico – We were responsible for public relations in the Southeastern United States for the country of Mexico.

- San Carlos Country Club, Guaymas, Mexico – Brought in by Roy Dye, Pete's cousin, we opened this golf and tennis community on the Sea of Corez.

- State of Merida, Venezuela. Working for the then-governor, William Davila, our task was to promote the incipient Agritourism program he initiated there.

- Amelia Island Plantation, Florida. We actually represented this environmentally advanced resort community in three different periods, the last one celebrating their 25th anniversary.

- Arvida resorts: Between 1971 and 1988, 17 years, we did the public relations for all of Arvida's Florida communities: Boca Raton Hotel & Club, Boca West, Broken Sound, Weston, Palm Beach Polo and Country Club, Sawgrass, and Longboat Key Club.

- Bal Harbour Shoppes, Florida. We were public relations consultants to Stan Whitman, founder of these tony shops in Bal Harbour.

- Chesterfield (Liggett Tobacco). We introduced this new pure-leaf cigarette for Liggett Tobacco, just prior to the time when owner Bennet Lebow settled the major industry-wide lawsuit.

- Collier Resources, Naples, Florida. We worked with this family and the South Florida environmental community to defeat the plan for a major new commercial airport at Homestead Air Force Base.

- Cocoplum, Coral Gables, Florida. Working with Florida Audubon, we helped achieve an agreement in this community which provided for 36 acres of native mangroves to be left in perpetuity.

- Fisher Island, Florida. We introduced this island resort and club community to the United States and then to Europe, where it was very well received.

- Deering Bay, Coral Gables, Florida. Retained by developers Armando Codina and Jeb Bush, we did the public relations for this bayside community for six years.

- Florida Chamber of Commerce, Tallahassee. We rolled out their "Pro Biz – No Biz" anti-regulatory campaign throughout the state.
- Graham for Governor Campaign. We did the public relations for Bob Graham's two campaigns for Governor, working with him primarily on environmental issues;

  - Save the Manatees
  - Save Our Everglades
  - Save Our Shoreline

We also wrote campaign speeches for Governors Lawton Chiles and Reuben Askew.

- Harbour Ridge, Florida. Working with developer John Dodge, we were able to help establish Harbour Ridge as an iconic conservation community, for which I received the President's Award of Florida Audubon Society in 1988.

- Nicklaus, Sierra Development Corp., Florida. We worked on two major golf communities in Louisiana for this company, English Turn, and Country Club of Louisiana.

- Northern Trust Banks of Florida. We were retained to help this Chicago-based company make the transition from a trust company to a bank, and to reach a younger demographic.

- Old Marsh Golf Club, Florida. Again, Pete Dye brought us in to promote his radically new environmental marsh/drainage system. This 250 member club has no starting times.

- PGA National Golf Club, Florida. Llwyd Ecclestone, Jr., son of Lost Tree Founder, Llwyd Ecclestone, brought us aboard to help promote this high quality golf community. We named his top golf course "The Champion."

- Ibis Golf and Country Club, Florida. Nearby Ibis, also developed by Llwyd, Jr., had three Nicklaus courses: the first by Jack, the second by son Jack II, and the third by son Steve.

- Sailfish Point, Florida. We were retained to publicize this oceanfront community's 25th anniversary, and the renovation of Jack Nicklaus' golf course.

- Seabrook Island, S. C. In doing the Public Relations for this outstanding barrier island community, we brought in Al Bunis and his Tennis Grand Masters, featuring some of the greatest names in the game: Pancho Gonzalez, Vic Seixas, Torben Ulrich and Sven Davidson.

- Silverado, California. Following the course built by his father, Robert Trent Jones, Jr. brought us in to create national interest in his new mountainside course.

- The Miami law firms of:

  - Broad & Cassel
  - Mershon, Sawyer

- Shea & Gould
- Katz, Barron, Squitero

- Hotel Mayfair House, Coconut Grove, Florida. For this unique art district property, we were able to bring in the Dave Letterman Show to broadcast from the hotel for five days.

- Windsor, Vero Beach, Florida. Once again recommended by golf architect Robert Trent Jones, Jr., we opened his course and the tennis complex at this Canadian-owned oceanfront community.

- Hualalai, Hawaii. Working for the Kawasaki Corporation, we developed the master marketing plan for this Four Seasons resort community and its Jack Nicklaus golf course.

- Huntsman Springs, Idaho. We established a national identity for this 1,500-acre family vacation community, including its amenities (golf, fly fishing, mountain trail, wellness center) and luxury homes.

- Desert Mountain, Arizona. Were instrumental in helping Lyle Anderson achieve the Golf Digest Top 100 list for his then-new Geronimo course – designed by his friend Jack.

- Bahia Beach, Puerto Rico. Helped the Sanchez family establish its new Robert Trent Jones, Jr. oceanfront golf course, its new St. Regis Hotel and Resort, and its array of real estate products.

- The Landings of Skidaway Island, Savannah, Georgia. Opened this island community with a Frank Duane/Arnold Palmer golf course.

- Pro Bono Service:
  - Miami Mega-City Special Olympics (Board Chairman)
  - St. Alban's Day Nursery (Board of Trustees)
  - Planned Parenthood of Miami (Video)
  - Shake-A-Leg Miami (Video)
  - Florida Audubon Society (President's Award, Board of Directors)
  - Tropical Audubon Society (Board of Directors)
  - International Foundation for Junior Golf (Celebrity Tournament)
  - Recreational Development Council, Urban Land Institute
  - Florida Endowment for the Humanities (Board of Directors)
  - Ransom-Everglades School (Board of Trustees)
  - Summit of the Americas Committee
  - We Will Rebuild Committee (Hurricane Andrew)
  - Junior Orange Bowl Committee (Annual Parade)
  - Dade County Grand Jury (Foreman)
  - American Red Cross (Board of Directors)
  - United States Golf Assn. (Communications Committee)
  - PGA of America (Ambassador Program)
  - YMCA of Greater Miami (Advisory Board)
  - University of Miami School of Nursing (Development)
  - University of Miami School of Architecture (Special Projects)
  - Good Hope Equestrian Training Center (Development)
  - Save the Manatee Committee (TV Public Service Campaign)

CLIENTS, EDITORS, COLLEAGUES

"When we worked together at Windsor (Vero Beach, FL) David and his team were a pleasure to work with. Their marketing and publicity efforts led to excellent results. To this day, we continue to benefit from David's sage advice and confidently recommend the David Pearson Associates team to developers in search of long term marketing vision and expert execution."

Marie Roberts – Co-Founder, Private Communities.com

"In 1970 I recommended David Pearson to Gulf + Western. He put my Teeth of the Dog golf course, and Casa de Campo, on the map. He and his son Chris also promoted Santa Barbara Plantation in Curacao, where my son P. B. and I designed a course. Alice says it's in the genes."

Pete Dye, Golf Course Architect

"For over thirty years I have known David Pearson as a strategic thinker with a crisp communications style. He has contributed to several of the most successful resort properties in the United States and the Caribbean. On the dark side, David has a profound interest and grasp of politics and my resume is the beneficiary. His friendship and wise counsel are personal treasures.

Former U. S. Senator Bob Graham

"Since I first worked with David Pearson when we shared Fisher Island as a client, through the excellent work his firm did with our tennis center at Landfall in North Carolina, I have nothing but respect for his firm. We are now working with his son Chris and a staff of talented professionals as we plan a new tennis complex in Panama. With the Pearsons on our team, we fully expect nothing less than a straight set victory."

Cliff Drysdale, Tennis Legend and Television Commentator

"Our association with David Pearson Associates is as strong today as it has been for over thirty years. Their competence, commitment and flexibility in performing their functions have opened many doors for us. The firm is very knowledgeable in public relations and strategic marketing, and the reputation they have established in the resort development industry over the years is impressive. Above all, we treasure the personal relationship that we have with David and Chris Pearson and the frankness with which they give us their advice."

Federico J. Sanchez-Ortiz, President and CEO, Interlink
Group LLC
Developers of Bahia Beach
Resort and Golf Club,
Puerto Rico

"David Pearson Associates has guided us through the tough development start-up period with their insights and expertise. From the strategic Marketing Plan and the PR campaign – contacting the most effective media and providing them with the right message – to improving the copy on some of tour advertising pieces, DPA has showed their talent strategically and tactically. We will continue partnering with the best in each field, and the folks at DPA are the prime example of a firm that creates value for its clients."

Gary Martin, Managing Director, Portones Del Mar Yacht Club and Resort, Panama

"David Pearson Associates understands the needs of individual media outlets better than any other marketing/public relations firm I have ever worked with. Like seasoned journalists, they know what makes a compelling story. As a result, I have written articles for Forbes Magazine about several of Pearson's clients over the years. I look forward to working with them again on many more articles to come."

Carrie Coolidge, Forbes, Pursuitist

"I have worked with David Pearson Associates for 26 years as a publisher and editor of several luxury lifestyle magazines. There is nobody better at the business of public relations and marketing. Not only do they combine great talent and creativity with expert travel, resort and real estate knowledge, but they are also terrific people. A world class team!"

Kevin Pickens, Publisher and Editor, The Golfer

"David Pearson Associates is always a pleasure to work with, and they are a trusted source of information on golf courses, resorts, private communities, and more. I know that when they call me, it's with something good."

Bruce Wallin, Group Editorial Director Robb Report

"Getting the world's attention requires a vast network of connections. David Pearson has connected me to some of the world's great resorts: Casa de Campo, Punta Mita, Reserva Conchal and Royal Westmoreland, to name a few."

Ralph Stewart Bowden, Publisher
Bowden's Market Barometer

David Pearson's life in and around media has been the equivalent of at least three lives, all of them worth examining (for many good reasons). His recollections are priceless.

John Underwood, author
"My Turn at Bat"
(with Ted Williams)

David and Anne Pearson